We Write

We Write

An anthology of prose and poetry by the **Write On Writers**
of People Plus in Brunswick, Maine © 2022

Other publications by the **Write On Writers** People Plus include:
Poets and Storytellers; Writing for fun
Poets and Storytellers; Writing for fun, volume II
It's about Time; Poems & Stories read by the authors
Muses and Memories; An Anthology of Prose and Poetry
From Maine and Away; An Anthology of Prose and Poetry
Times and Seasons, Writings from the Heart of Maine
    An Anthology of Prose and Poetry
Journeys and Reflections
Out of Our Minds
Write From the Heart

Design & Cover by Paul Karwowski
Free Cover Illustration courtesy of Vecteezy.com
Illustrations by the People Plus Art Class
Publication by People Plus

ACKNOWLEDGEMENTS

A special recognition is in order for the following people who made this publication possible:

The members for assuming the role of facilitator for the group on a rotating basis for the past year,

Paul Karwowski for his efforts in the organization, editing, and arrangement of this book,

Ed Higgins and the People Plus Art Class for their delightful and colorful illustrations contained in this book,

Robert Mulligan for proof reading the final draft of this book,

Paul Karwowski, Fred Cheney, and Bill Perry for proof reading the proof book,

And Executive Director Stacy Frizzle-Edgerton and Marketing Coordinator Jennifer Felkay for their efforts in its publication.

The *Write On Writers* would also like to express its appreciation to Executive Director Stacy Frizzle-Edgerton and the Staff of People Plus for their past and continuing efforts on the group's behalf.

IN MEMORY
Ralph Neil Laughlin

Ralph was a University of Iowa graduate. Upon graduation he joined General Electric's Marketing Communications Department (advertising group). After twelve years with GE, he went on to work for other industry leaders.

He authored seven books, the latest being *Scribblings – The Brunswick Years*, a compendium of prose and poetry done while living in Brunswick.

He and Dianne, his wife of fifty-five plus years, resided in New Orleans, LA for the past year, yet retained strong ties to Maine. Their three grown children live and work around the globe.

Other Books include: *Beyond The Pool, The Day The World Cried As One, Random Thoughts of A Wandering Mind, 1,001 Bites of Chinese Fortune Cookie Wisdom, Food For Thought…In The Bed, And Tarzan: The Greystoke Legacy Under Siege.* All available on Amazon books.

Ralph was a member of People Plus for 8 years. He volunteered in the kitchen for the men's and lady's breakfasts, monthly lunches, Thanksgiving dinner, and parties. He was known as Frank's "Wingman."

Ralph was a valued member and contributor to ***Write On Writers***. In addition to his own books and writings, he mentored and aided other writers in the group with the publication of their books. He and his wife, Dianne, also started Books A La Carte, a group of readers who meet to discuss books at People Plus.

Even though they moved to Louisiana to be close to their family, Ralph still sent his writings to be read at the group's meetings. He will be sincerely missed at our table.

TIME

The Past is Memory.
Don't let it haunt you.
The Future is speculation.
Don't let it scare you.
The Present is now.
Live it. Embrace it.
Life is too short
To do anything else.

A BLESSING

On
Your Life's Journey
may you have enough ...
Hope
to make you motivated,
Trials
to make you strong,
Sorrow
to make you human,
and
Happiness
to make you joyous.

SOLACE

Today, your tears of mourning
will nourish the seeds of memory,
bringing forth serene-scented
blossoms of remembrances
that will fill your heart with
warm thoughts.

DEDICATION

This book is dedicated to those who love words and appreciate the skill, and sometimes magic, it takes to turn those words into something you'll never forget. We love sharing our words with each other in the **Write On Writers** of People Plus, and now we're happy to share them with you.

CONTENTS

AUTHORS .... PAGE

Bonnie Wheeler 1
Vince McDermott 12
Gladys Szabo 19
Paul Karwowski 28
Sally Hartikka 41
Betty Bavor 52
Russ Kinne 64
Nonie Moody 69
Ginny Sabin 78
Wayne Mogk 85
Lucy Derbyshire 96
Doris Weinberg 101
Bill Perry 114
Carol Markell 128
Robert Mulligan 141
Christa Kay 154
Alene Staley 166

ILLUSTRATOR LIST

ARTIST	SUBJECT	PAGE
Lauralee Poutree	Quill	2
	Cookies	4
	Squirrel	13
	Miss Muffet	17
	Dog blanket	22
	Dog bed	22
	Bluebird	46
	Ink pen and well	67
	Fisherman	79
	Design	80
	Trees	82
	Toy	92
	Jumprope	104
	Jacks	104
	Whistle	108
	Nest	167
	Lady slipper	169
	Baby ducks	170
Nancy Pantaz	Parakeet	3
	Teacher	5
	Bag of snacks	21
	Socks	35
	Oasis	38
	Thinking man	65
	Lightbulb	94
	Pancakes	98
	Old car	109

	Grandma	112
	Letter	150
	Halloween	162
Ann Frey	Cane	7
	Swing	10
	Mask	23
	Phone	33
	Fire helmet	48
	Buoy	59
	Rocker	73
	Nest	83
	Dancing	84
	Plane	86
	Pointed shoe	92
	Snake	99
	Apple	108
	Medal	113
	Canoe	130
	Computer	155
	Seagull	156
	Coffee	165
Jen Haskins	Cupcake	18
	Tree	146
	Butterfly	147
Beth Miller	Harp	29
	Typewriter	40
	Toboggan	71
	Camera	138

Allison Coffin	Sailboat..................................37
	Campfire...............................56
	Clock......................................77
Ed Higgins	Helicopter............................45
	Maine staycation 49
	Crashed spaceship 87
	Chipmunk...........................168
Ann Sanfasin	Soapbox racer.......................55
Tony Lacroix	Boat..53
Susan Morris	Rain 47
	Mittens................................160
Myrtle Lacroix	Rabbit....................................97
	Maple leaf...........................102
Richard Nickerson	Waterfall.............................131

INTRODUCTION

The members of the *Write On Writers* of People Plus are thrilled to bring you our ninth publication of poetry, humor, prose (fiction and non-fiction), memoirs, and other delightful wonders. We are especially pleased to have the People Plus Art Class join us in this endeavor with their creative illustrations.

Mysteries will make you search for an answer in "The Harp" and "The Question." Surely, "Where There Is Smoke" will get your attention. You will get an understanding of why we writers write from a few authors in "Why I Write," "I Write," and "On Writing."

Heart-felt memoirs like "Porch Swing" and "My Favorite Teacher," or "Lunch with A Seagull" may make you recall similar experiences in your own life, or maybe the thrill of a "Wednesday Afternoon Sled Ride" will do the same.

Find a little state history in "The Year Maine Burned," or learn about volunteering in "Volunteers," or scouting in "Yes, I Am Still A Girl Scout" and "March Is Girl Scout Cookies."

You can't avoid the little bits of humor in "Drive Left" and "Strange Phone Calls," and "Maple Syrup." For deeper and more thoughtful reading delve into the poetry of "The Sea So Wide," "Life Meanings," and "Make Believe Sky," or "A Special Tree" and "Bravery Takes Courage," along with "Nature" and "The Written Letter."

For animal lovers there is a treasure trove of reading in "Life with Woody," "Calleigh," "My Grady," and "A Dog's Love," or for those into wild animals there is "Avian and Human Nesting Habits," "Chipmunks," and "Here Come the Crows."

Welcome, kind readers. I have given you titles of a small sample of writings of all kinds in this book. We do hope you enjoy reading these stories and poems as much as we have enjoyed writing them.

Paul Karwowski
For the *Write On Writers*

Bonnie Wheeler

Bonnie spent her childhood playing in the red dirt of Oklahoma. Today she spends her senior years playing in the snow in Maine. She shares her love of writing in a variety of styles. Fiction, non-fiction, and short stories.

She has self-published two books, *Without My Toothbrush* and *Mama's Pies*. She has been published in magazines, newspapers and fence posts, as well as many anthologies.

Her greatest achievement is Mom to three children, Brad, Kevin and Lonna; nine grandchildren; and six great-grandchildren, all perfect in her eyes. She is grateful, hopeful, and at peace with God.

Bonnie Wheeler

I WRITE

I write to soothe my soul.
I write boldly, so I am told.
Words flow about love, laughter, and strife.
Words flow about family, friends, and life.
The gift empowered by a hand I do not see
Satisfaction rains, when inspiration falls on me.
I write…

I LOVE YOU
BRAD-KEVIN-LONNA

I loved you when I felt you kick inside
And when you learned to talk.
I loved you at your very first cry
And when you learned to walk.

I loved you when you started first grade
And graduated for all to see,
And made your way into a difficult world
To begin your new life without me.

I loved you when you walked the aisle
And chose a special partner for life.
And when all those grandchildren came,
It brought more love into my life.

I love the joy they add to my life,
Each special in their own way,
And another gift as great-grandchildren arrive,
A blessing I never dreamed I say.

So now is the time to tell you,
You all grow more precious each day,
To remind you of the love, as I held you in my arms,
Is the same love that I hold in my heart today.

Bonnie Wheeler

TOPAZ

The kids wanted a pet, so my neighbor, who was moving and couldn't take hers with her, gave it to them. It was a yellow parakeet named Topaz. We tamed him pretty easily. He was a very smart bird.

Topaz began to talk in sentences. Some of the first things he said were, "Close the door"; "Brad, go to your room"; and "Pretty bird." He imitated each of our voices and we could tell who he was imitating.

He also figured out how to open his cage and then fly to wherever he wanted to go. This did not please us, so we began locking his cage with a clothespin. Topaz lived with us for several years.

Since we were a military family, eventually the time came for us to move as we were transferred across the country from California to Maine. The kids threw a fit when we told them that we wouldn't be able to take Topaz with us because we would be traveling in the winter and the plan was to sleep in the pickup camper. It would be too cold for the bird.

After weeks of pleading and begging from the kids, we finally gave in but said, "Ok, if it dies on the way, don't say we didn't warn you."

Sure enough, it was freezing when we stopped to sleep. We knew the bird would not survive in the cage, so we took Topaz out and held him under the blankets all night He pecked and tried to get away. It was not a fun or restful night, yet we all survived, including Topaz. He went on with us to visit our parents in Oklahoma and Texas and became a well-traveled Navy bird.

Bonnie Wheeler

COOKIES

My favorite cookie
I really love them all
Whether soft or crunchy
I love them big or small

Chocolate or vanilla
With nuts or chocolate chips
I can't resist the flavor
As they pass by my willing lips

And if I eat too many
As I usually do
My blood sugar rises
Oh dear, what's a diabetic to do?

BRITTANY

She snuggles under a family quilt
Old family names faded and faint
Great grandma Ruby held the thread that binds
That linked our family in good and bad times
Spreading her warmth and love
Through three generations of her blood.

Bonnie Wheeler

MY FAVORITE TEACHER

She looked like a movie star. Like Jane Russell, she was tall, lots of dark hair, well dressed, lots of jewelry, and perfect makeup with dark wet red lipstick. If you stood close to her, a warm sweet scent of Tabu perfume engulfed you and if you walked by her classroom, the fragrance would draw you in. Mrs. Morgan was my favorite teacher. I loved to just sit and look at her.

Being extremely shy, I could have easily been overlooked in her speech class. She would find ways to make me take part in class and make me feel special. She encouraged me to go beyond what I thought I could do. She chose me to represent our school in a speech contest in Oklahoma City. I said, "No! She said, "Yes."

I truly thought I would die or at least faint and fall off the stage, but with my eyes on her, I delivered the speech and got a high mark. – Life lesson – You are successful if you don't faint and fall off the stage. It served me well my whole life.

Mrs. Morgan gently pulled more from me than I dreamed I could give. For me, she set an example of how to look, act, care, and encourage, and also how to smell. If you don't believe me, smell my Tabu perfume. It was the first bottle of perfume I purchased when I graduated from high school and got a job. After all these years I still keep a bottle to remind me of that special teacher who knew I could fly and gave me a loving push into all my tomorrows.

Bonnie Wheeler

GOOD MORNING

Time to rise and shine
Time to bloom where you are planted
A world so vast – experience it fully
in a blink of an eye
Time drips away like warm honey

WHO?

Who understands when your mood is bad?
Who listens when you're really sad?
Who advises a new road to take?
Who takes you to the doctor when you ache?
Who washes the floor when you throw up?
Who says to your face? You need to – grow up.
You see the love shining through.

Only a mother, that's who.

MEMORIES

Do you remember
When we were we?
Now, you are you
And I am me.

Do you remember
When babies were born
And we were all we?
Now, they are they
And you are you
And I am me.

Sweet memories
Of when we were us.

Bonnie Wheeler

FALL IN NEW ENGLAND

Fall color lights the world
Forest green, deep scarlet reds
And glorious golds

In the darkness of life
We are enveloped in light
Created by the Master

The wonder of the beauty
Fills our being
We breath it into our souls with gratitude

HARVEST TIME

The harvest of my life
Years waiting to receive it
Childhood, teen years
Motherhood, and menopause
Survived it all in a blur

I'm ready to slow down
To take care of no one but myself
I can at last say NO!
To the world's requests

I can enjoy my talents
Savor moments of silence
Listening, feeling
Hardly breathing

The adventures of a new beginning
Now is my time
My personal harvest
It's about time

Bonnie Wheeler

THE BOOK

Rushing through the Cincinnati airport to make my connecting flight to Maine, I stopped in at the restroom. I noticed a book on top of the paper holder. I turned around and asked the few women in the restroom, "Did anyone leave this book?" No one had. What to do? If it wasn't mine, should I put it back? I thought, "This is an airport. No one will fly back to claim it." I decided to turn it in.

I walked out and spoke to an airport official. "I found this book," I said and handed it to him. "You can turn it into the Information Desk," he told me and gave me elaborate directions. Well, it was the opposite direction of my outgoing flight, but I started walking in the direction he gave me. My knees were hurting, I was hungry. I was thinking, "This book is not worth all this trouble. They will probably throw it away." So, I turned around and headed for my gate, grabbing a hot dog on the way.

After checking in, I sat down to rest and eat my hot dog. Then I heard the intercom announcement, the one I had been hearing over and over about not taking anything from anyone to carry on the airplane or leaving luggage unattended. Oh, my Lord.
Did someone leave that book on purpose with a bomb in it? Could that happen? I looked suspiciously at the book now sitting beside me in an empty chair. I had even told an airport employee that I had picked it up. Were they watching me? Was security coming any minute to take the book and me into custody? Was I going to miss my flight? Maybe I should leave it on the seat and walk away. Oh dear, that may look more suspicious.

I picked up the book and really looked at it for the first time. It was brand new and the title was *Living Serendipitously*. I couldn't help it; I just began to laugh. I knew that word meant living in the moment, expecting wonderful things to happen. Einstein said that there are two ways to live life: as though nothing is a miracle or as though everything is a miracle. I heard my flight called. I tucked the book under my arm and boarded the plane for home.

Bonnie Wheeler

MY WORST JOB EVER

The worst job I ever had was pulling cotton. I had an uncle who was a farmer. He needed the crops brought in to the gin. School was closed so all the children could help.

We got up with the sun, put on old clothes and gloves. Then we picked up a cotton sack and out we rode to the farm where row upon row of cotton grew. I put the cotton sack over my shoulder, bent over, pulled row after row of cotton bolls and threw them into the sack. When the sack was as full as I could drag it, it was weighed, recorded, and emptied into the cotton trailer, and then, back I went to pick another sack full.

It was hot, sweaty, hard work. My back hurt, my hands got cut up, and I would die for a cool drink of water. At sundown, I was done, Hallelujah! It was a job I would only do again if my kids were starving.

TREES

Over 100 years old
Strong and tall
Shading the world
Different generations
Looking up
Over time
Where did they go

Bonnie Wheeler

PORCH SWING

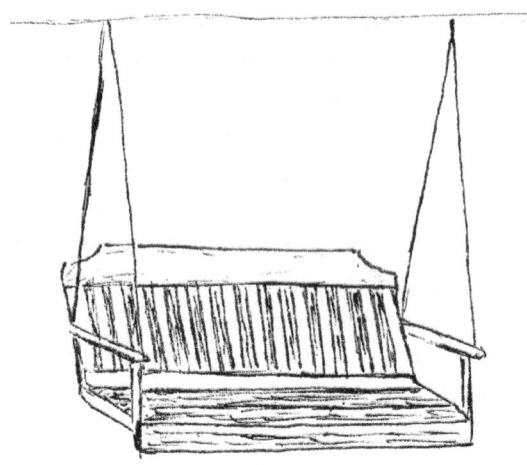

Dad and I sat on the front porch swing. He asked me again, "Where do you live, Hon?"

I answered for the fourth time, "Dad, I live in Maine."

He thought about it and five minutes later he asked me again, "Hon, where do you live?"

This time I repeated louder, "In Maine, Dad, in Maine."

I told him that I was going to help Mother in the kitchen and stomped off. He just sat there and stared into the empty yard.

I heard Mom humming as she stirred soup in a black pot.

"Mom, how do you stand it?

"Your dad has Alzheimer's," she says.

"I know that Mom, but doesn't it drive you crazy when he asks the same thing over and over? "

She looked at me, "I remember after a hard day's work some little girl," she paused and gave a knowing look, "would grab his hand and take him outside to see a rainbow and start asking questions.

"Daddy, what makes the different colors? Why does it make a circle? What keeps it up there? Is it part of the sky? Where does it go when it disappears? Will we ever see it again? Do the stars ever fall down?"

Bonnie Wheeler

"Daddy, when we have another tornado can I stand outside the cellar and watch it with you? Will it pick us up in a tree like we saw the blanket after the last tornado? If you hold my hand, I will be safe."

"Yes, I remember." I turned and went back to the porch swing. I sat down and took Dad's hand and said, "Dad, let me tell you about where I live in Maine, near the ocean. You and Mom came to see me once and you went deep sea fishing. You had the best time catching all those fish."

We both smiled…

WORDS

Sweet words
Eager ears
Harsh words
Silent tears

Vince McDermott

Vince was born in Trenton, NJ. He lived in many locations as a military dependent and while serving in the USAF for nine years. He and his wife, Joanne (a Brunswick native), moved to Maine in 1998. He was a meteorologist for over thirty years, serving in the Air Force and working for the National Weather Service and in private industry.

Vince wrote many nonfiction articles prior to joining the ***Write On Writers*** in 2005. He now writes historical fiction, tales about strange happenings, poetry, and stories about life in Maine. He has contributed pieces to magazines and has recited poetry at readings.

Vince McDermott

SQUIRRELS

It was a bright, warm early spring day. Kevin Tillman sat at his desk trying to think about something to write. He glanced out the window. He had been cooped up for some time due to COVID and bad weather. He noticed a small squirrel leaping from tree branch to tree branch. He had never seen one fall to the ground during leaps. Another squirrel joined the first. Oh, well, back to work.

He typed a few trial sentences, then gave up. He looked out at the trees again. Now there were three, no – four squirrels there. He had not seen that many all winter. Maybe there had been a bumper crop of babies. He glanced at the ground. There were more squirrels there. It looked as if he might have to trap some and transport them across the river. He often wondered if any he had trapped in the past had ever made it back to his yard.

Some of the squirrels saw him looking out at them. They stared at him. One moved toward the house. Others followed. He remembered that he had not shut his garage door. Varmints liked to go in there. He went out through the mud room and reached out to close the door. There were squirrels in the garage. He did not want to shut them in since they could cause damage when they tried to escape. He decided to leave the door open and started back to his den.

It was such a fine day that he opened a window a little on the way to let in fresh air. He was about to sit down when he remembered that he had not put his screens in yet. The squirrels might get in. He rushed back to the window and almost stepped on a squirrel. More squirrels came through the window. Now what? If he closed the window, the squirrels would be trapped. As he hesitated, one of the critters leaped at him. He fell backward and stepped on another squirrel. He lost his balance and crashed to the floor. Other squirrels jumped on him. He felt them biting and tearing at his flesh. He knocked some away, but others joined in the carnage. He tried to get up, but slipped again. His head hit a table and he passed out. The squirrels moved in for the kill.

Vince McDermott

A SHORT MYSTERY

Inspector Carstairs had a big problem. Lady Penelope Farnham was killed in what at first appeared to be a robbery gone wrong. A few items were taken and the room where her body was found had been ransacked, but several valuable pieces were still there. So, if a robbery didn't happen, why was she killed? She was a widow in her eighties with no children. She was well off, but not extremely wealthy. Nevertheless, Carstairs had to look at money as a motive. One of his first tasks was to get a look at Lady Penelope's will. The will showed that five people benefitted from her death. When he questioned the five, he found out that Lady Penelope had been very open about telling people that those close to her would be "taken care of."

The five were: Millie, the maid, Cranford, the butler, Cecily Hargraves, a lifelong neighbor and friend, Dr. Forbes, and Derek Ogilvie, a cousin. Millie had been employed for about five years. She spent her earnings as fast as she received them. Cranford had been in service for about 20 years. He wanted to retire, but needed money to build a cottage. Cecily had never been rich. Dr. Forbes had been taking care of Penelope for many years and had said that she had some years yet ahead of her. He gambled. And Derick, who lived in a not too prosperous part of London, said he had not seen his cousin in years.

Lady Penelope had lived in Berwick, a small town on the rail line between London and Dover. Carstairs, an avid reader of detective stories, decided to try a familiar trick. He would gather the five in a room and see if he could trip one up. After several hours of questioning, he was getting nowhere. He was about to give up and send them home when a train whistle sounded. Derek, a know-it-all, piped up and remarked "that must be the 11:10 to London." Carstairs jumped on that. "Now how did you know that, sir? The 11:10 service only started a year ago. You must have been down here since then." The inspector had his man.

Vince McDermott

HICKORY, DICKORY, DOCK

Hickory, Dickory, Dock. The mouse ran up the clock. Let's hit the pause button here. Why would a mouse run up a clock? We are not told. What kind of clock is it? We aren't told that either. The clock struck one. Down the mouse ran (or run) there are a number of versions of the rhyme. Does anything about the rhyme make sense? Possibly.

There is one theory that the clock refers to a big one in Exeter Cathedral in England. There was a cat door in the clock which allowed a cat to chase mice. So, it is possible that a mouse ran up the clock to escape a cat and ran down when scared by the clock striking one.

THE ZOO

I had been to the zoo many times when I was a child. I was thrilled by the exhibits. But, as time progressed, I lost interest in the same old sights. As I grew older, I visited the zoo less often.

Then I became intrigued by the announcement that a new exhibit was being shown. I went to the zoo with some misgivings. I was not impressed by the entrance and the first cages I passed. There had been no changes. I almost decided to leave when I noticed a banner which proclaimed that the new exhibit was ahead. I hesitated, but, since I was there, I went on. I passed under the banner and approached the cage. I was really disappointed. What a disgusting exhibit! A pale, thin being with no outstanding features. All it did was eat, scream, and crash against its cage. As I left, I looked back at the sign identifying the species. It read:
HOMO SAPIENS

Vince McDermott

HOW COULD I FORGET?

How could I forget what's her name? She was my first real flame. Eyes of blue. Always to me true. Long black hair not subject to very much care. Small and thin. A dimple in her chin. Always well dressed. With style she was blessed. I thought she was the prettiest girl alive when we were both five.

THE QUESTION

The book collector approached the door. It was a plain door, white, set in a white frame. It was surrounded by a whitish haze. It seemed as if he had no choice but to open it. He grasped the handle and pulled it down. The door opened silently. He stepped into a room. His mouth opened in awe. It was the most sumptuously decorated room he had ever seen. A cheery fire was burning in a large fireplace. A table was set in front of it laden with a selection of the finest food. Bottles of great wine were on the table.

Then a door opened. The most beautiful woman he had ever seen walked in. She walked to the table, poured two glasses of wine and handed one to him. He was about to drink when he noticed something in this wonderful room – there were no bookcases! He could not understand that. He asked the woman why there no books in the room. She pointed to a small table. There was one book on it. He hurried over to it, completely ignoring the woman, the food, and the wine. It had to be the greatest, most treasured book in the world. The book was very, very old. The cover was flaking. He opened it and began to read. He read a few pages, then hurried on to others. He looked up in horror. It was awful – complete drivel – possibly the worst book ever written. What is going on?

Question – is he in heaven or is he in hell?

Vince McDermott

REVISED NURSERY RHYMES

Jack and Jill went up the hill to fetch a pail of water.

Up a hill to get water? If you believe that, I've got some bottom land you might be interested in. They came down 90 minutes later – without the water. We shall not go into what happened up there. Then they encountered

Little Miss Muffet who sat on a tuffet eating curds and whey, when along came a spider.

"Little" – hah. She flattened the poor tuffet. As she scarfed up her disgusting dish, the poor spider blundered into it. Miss Muffet didn't miss a beat. She ate the whole mess.

Jack and Jill ran off down the lane and met an old woman who lived in a shoe. She had so many children, she didn't know what to do.

It is obvious she didn't know what to do. If she did, she would not have had so many children. No wonder she looked old. She was only thirty-two.

Vince McDermott

POETRY, MUSIC, AND CUPCAKES

Poetry and music
A good combination
Soothes the soul
I look around the room
I bet those cupcakes are delicious

Some poetry is light and entertaining
Some is serious
I relax
But am brought back to reality
I can't take my eyes off the cupcakes

I try to pay attention
Concentrate on the readings
Enjoy the tunes
But it is hard
Are people taking the cupcakes?

The last reader is finished
The music is winding down
People are moving to the back
Headed for the cupcakes
I better move fast

Success! I have one. It has been a good evening

Gladys Szabo

Gladys was born in Jamaica, New York, moved to Connecticut at the age of one, and then to Maine in 2000. She has two children, Robert, and Dawn, and four granddaughters.

While raising her family, Gladys was active in Boy Scouts and Girl Scouts, and continues with Girl Scouting as a leader going on her 42nd year. She has also been an Angel with the Maine State Music Theater for 5 yrs., adopting an intern each year, ushering, and helping the performers.

Working for Independence Association was an important part of her life since she moved to Maine. It was more than just a job. She made several very close personal relationships with people, some of whom remain in her life as extended family.

Her greatest joys are her family, friends, pets, and meeting new people. Her passion for animals, crafts, and volunteering are the focus for most of her writing,

Writing has always been a hobby for Gladys and was the reason she joined the ***Write On Writers*** in 2009. Since becoming a member, she has expanded her creativity and writing techniques, and is also working on her memoirs.

She is currently in the process of moving back to Connecticut where she will be closer to more family. This is both a sad and happy move, regretting leaving all her wonderful connections here but happy to be closer to family.

Gladys Szabo

SHOPLIFTER

Elizabeth is down and out! She lost her job due to lack of business. She has two children, Keily, 5, and Kevin, 8. She is an honest person, but when it comes to family, she will do anything for them. She decides to go to a grocery store in another neighborhood where she is not known. Carrying a shopping bag, puts on her mask, which is mandated, then she and Kiely go into the store while Kevin waits outside. Kiely is also carrying a smaller shopping bag. As they stroll down the aisles, Elizabeth nudges Kiely and eyes a product, and Kiely then glances around to check to see if anyone is looking and slips the item into her small bag. They continue through the store picking up several items. Elizabeth takes off the shawl she has over her shoulder and puts it in the bag covering half the items in the basket as they approach the cashier. Elizabeth tells Kiely, "Go wait outside with your brother while I check out."

The cashier starts to check out Elizabeth's items. As she nears the end, she becomes suspicious as the small number of items doesn't seem to empty the bag. Not wanting to make a scene, the cashier asks those waiting in the line to go to another cashier as she needs to close out her register. Now alone with Elizabeth she gently leans over the counter and quietly says "I feel you have several more items in your bag. Am I correct?"

Elizabeth freezes in place, her eyes fill with tears. The cashier closes her register asking Elizabeth, "Will you please follow me to my office?"

By now Elizabeth is terrified, not knowing if she should follow the cashier or make a run for it. Thinking about her children, she starts to run, crying hysterically and shaking so that she could hardly run while saying "I can't go with you, I have two children waiting outside for me!" The cashier steps in front of her and motions to the children to come with their mother.

Once in the office, the door is closed, the cashier asks Elizabeth to sit down and hands her a box of Kleenex. Looking at the children sitting on the floor hanging on to their mother's dress with terrifying fright in their little eyes, breaks the cashier's heart. She has some fruit and snacks she brought for her lunch and hands them to Kevin and Keily. They look to their mother for approval and Mom nods that it is okay.

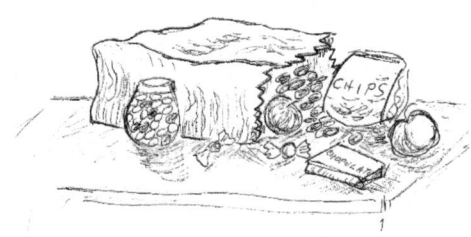

The cashier explains she isn't going to call the police and watches Elizabeth sigh with relief, sobbing while blurting out "I am so very sorry. Thank you for the fruit. My children haven't eaten since yesterday morning. I am desperate. I lost my job and am trying to care for my children so they are not taken away from me."

Now the cashier has tears in her eyes thinking of her own children and what she would do in this position. She asks Elizabeth if she would do her a favor.

Elizabeth is shocked, "What could I possibly do for you when I can't even take care of my family?"

"I am the owner of this store. I need someone to stock shelves. If you can do this your children can come with you and help, or stay in the back areas and play. I also run a pantry for people like yourself to get free food and other necessities. Promise me you will never try to steal again and will seek help from the authorities who can help you."

Elizabeth looked down at her children and burst into sobs. "Thank you, God, for sending this angel." Then she got up on her weak and shaking legs and hugged the cashier as she felt her children's arms around both while tears ran down their cute cheeks.

Gladys Szabo

THE CHRISTMAS BLANKET

Working for Independence Association, my first job was caring for Chuck, who lived with his parents. Chuck was not verbal and confined to a wheelchair, but we learned to communicate very well. I would get him up, dressed, fed, and then take him to the IA day program. Years later as his parents aged, I became co-guardian with his dad.

One Christmas I gave Chuck a warm furry throw with two large golden retrievers covering the whole blanket. Chuck loved dogs. When he would visit us, he would sit with his hand on one of our golden retriever's head. The dog never moved. The blanket became his favorite thing to always have with him. It went everywhere with him. When Chuck took his last breath, he had his blanket. I kept the blanket on my bedroom chair, reminding me of the 17 years we had together.

This past year I had to have my 16-year-old dog put down. I then adopted Hunter who was a rescue from Alabama.

While awaiting his arrival, I was preparing a crate and looking for bedding, when I noticed the blanket and thought, Chuck would love my dog having his blanket. I put it in the crate and fluffed it up.

Once Hunter was settled in, he would lie in the crate on his nice blanket while I made the bed and got dressed. When warmer weather came, I removed the blanket and put in lighter bedding. I realized that Hunter would lie on the floor in front of the crate while I did my morning chores, not in the crate. Now that the weather is cool again, I returned the blanket to the crate. This morning Hunter was lying in the crate while I made the bed.

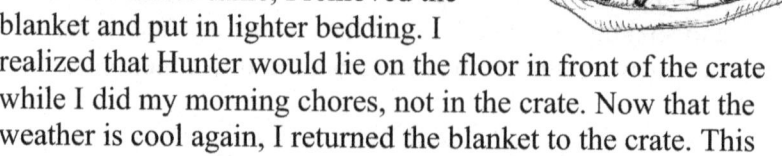

I like to think that maybe Hunter feels the love and connection Chuck and I had, and hope Chuck is smiling down on us.

Gladys Szabo

A SPECIAL MONTHLY LUNCH

After doing monthly lunches for twelve years, the interruption by the pandemic was heart breaking.

Frank and I, along with many special volunteers, worked together every month to prepare a lunch for 70 plus staff and volunteers. We shopped, chopped, served, and cleaned everything. Along with joys of accomplishments, we shared many tears over the losses of some of our wonderful volunteers. I looked forward every month to planning the meal, shopping with Frank, preparing the food, making favors, and centerpieces. Seeing all the people who came to enjoy the meal and socialize with friends old and new was the icing on the cake! I hugged each one as I called the tables.

Then Frank retired – lunches were still fun, but many adjustments had to be made. Frank was the core of the lunch! The pandemic reduced and finally we were able to have our monthly lunches as they were. Stacy and her staff did a fantastic job of keeping lunches going outside – all winter long. They were not the same but most importantly it kept everyone together to socialize. Things got to the point where we could eat inside 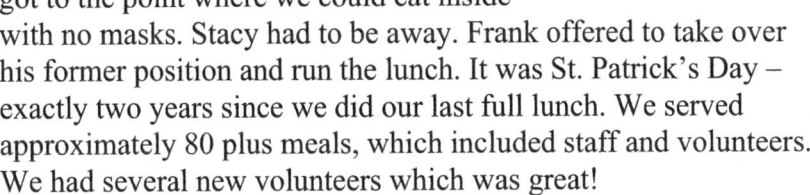 with no masks. Stacy had to be away. Frank offered to take over his former position and run the lunch. It was St. Patrick's Day – exactly two years since we did our last full lunch. We served approximately 80 plus meals, which included staff and volunteers. We had several new volunteers which was great!

I went home with tears of joy and a very happy heart. Since I am leaving in June, I feel I will never have this special lunch with Frank at the helm and our longtime volunteer people whom I haven't seen in two years. Only thing missing were the hugs – we still practiced safety. But the smiles and laughter certainly made the day a very special event. Something I will always hold in my heart forever.

Gladys Szabo

MARCH IS GIRL SCOUT COOKIES

Have you ever wondered
How Girl Scout Cookies get to you?
Cookies, Cookies by the ton
Each case handled one by one!
Unload the truck, stack five high
By kinds, by troop, with watchful eye.
Now break down cases and divide
Place extra boxes where implied.
Troops pick up and count again
If all correct, we say Amen.
Now scouts their boxes to be sorted
To their customers will be deported.
This may sound like a simple feat
But when all done, we are beat.
(Two thousand one hundred seventy-two cases
Is twenty-six thousand sixty-four boxes.)
Next come booth sales every weekend
Hundreds of scouts on sidewalks ascend.
Business lessons they are learning
While money they are gladly earning
Meeting goals the troop has set
Now fun and travel will onset.

VOLUNTEERS

Volunteers are the heart
of many places
Putting smiles on numerous faces
Helping others in various ways
Taking time out of their busy days
Doing for others is their goal
They deserve a badge of gold
For multiple tasks each one of you do
Our hearts overflow with
THANKS to you!

Gladys Szabo

CONTEMPLATING THOUGHTS FOR MY GRANDCHILDREN

My life was blessed the day you were born
Now proud of the woman into whom
you've transformed
As a college graduate, and are out on your own
Always remember you are never alone
Embrace the world with your beautiful smile
As you learn to develop your own lifestyle
Trust your inner most feelings
Don't be swayed by others pleading
Take well thought chances
On your way to advancement
Express your feeling but always be kind
Let it be the way you are defined
Remember it isn't the words that you say
But the manner in which they are said
Words said in anger cannot be reclaimed
Hurt feeling will always remain
Don't hold grudges
or be quick to make judgements
Admit when you are wrong and learn from mistakes
Create memories you will hold forever in your heart
And with your family never depart

HUGS AND SMILES

Hugs and smiles are most important
in my life.
I share them with care not thinking twice.
Now smiles are hidden behind a mask.
How can I show I care; I ask?
Social distancing, so we cannot touch.
Personal touch can intend so much.
Expressing warm and caring feelings,
Many times, are very healing.
Please wear masks, distance, and scrub
So before very long, again we can hug.

Gladys Szabo

AS I MOVE TO NEW ADVENTURES

As I review my past 12 years of being part of People Plus, I think of all I have done: playing games at Bath Senior center, going out to lunch with the monthly lunch group, enjoying hours with new and old friends at Sage Square Dance club, sharing writings with weekly **Write On Writers**, and attending many events such as Frank's monthly trips and others.

As a volunteer, I coordinated monthly lunches and desk receptionists, organized monthly lunch out, was an Angel and usher with Maine State Music Theater, plus a Girl Scout leader.

My point is not to show what I have done but to acknowledge how many people from all walks of life have touched my life every week. Many people overlap, others for just one event.

I am overwhelmed to think of the numerous people, different in so many ways, who made my life so full. I witnessed caring people willing to get along in group decisions, and wonder why the rest of the world can't do that. Perfect? No! Not at all. When people are willing to try to understand where another person is coming from and work through situations, amazing things are accomplished.

I was employed with Independence Association which aids physically and mentally challenged people of all ages. There is much to be learned from people who struggle with disabilities of all kinds as they are most loving and caring.

We need to think before we speak, keep a calm tone, and evaluate a situation before acting. Our world is in a difficult place. Changes can happen by teaching others to have respect for one another by working together towards one goal. We need to start with our youth, teaching them the things we were taught regarding respect, helping, and being kind to one another. Learning to agree or disagree and move on. Talk about situations, but when it's something you disagree with or really don't want to work out, walk away!

As I am now moving and leaving all these wonderful experiences behind, I am extremely sad. Life moves on and I am thrilled to be with family, which is most important. They are so supportive and loving and I thank them for all they do for me. Leaving Brunswick, People Plus and all the wonderful people who have given me so much love and true friendships is very difficult

I will make every effort to keep in touch and for sure will hold all of you in my heart. I am extremely thankful to have so many wonderful memories with so many special people and thank each of you for being one of those wonderful people!

I love giving hugs, so I leave a hug for each one of you.

Love and hugs.

MY AWAKENINGS

The morning was flawless
The sun shown on the dew drops
The trees dazzled with crystals
I was mesmerized
Young birds darted short distances
as playing on a playground
Chirping sounding like a choir,
sparrows, finches, and chickadees
Swooped across the yard
Some flew to the ground
Unable to get from tree to tree
Crows glided high above
Appearing to oversee the activity
As Noel, my dog, basked in the sun
Suggesting we linger a bit
Two small birds, dropped to my feet
As I observed them feeding one another
Or were they kissing?
Suddenly a serene feeling overcame me
I was awakened to what I was missing
Since I removed my feeders
The antics of chipmunks and squirrels outside the window
Driving my pets to a frenzy
Feeders returned – pets will adjust

Paul Karwowski (P.K. Allen)

Paul with son Tony, his wife, Danielle, and grandsons Griffin and Seth ready to go wilderness camping in California.

Paul Karwowski (pen name P.K. Allen) was born and raised in New Jersey. He served in the Navy in Patrol Squadron 26 in Brunswick, Maine. It was in Brunswick that he met his wife of 45 years, Pinky (Margaret). They built a home in Topsham in 1971 where they raised two boys, Peter and Anthony, and a girl, Amy. Since Amy was handicapped, they became involved with parent groups at Pineland and at the State level.

Amy died in 1996, and Pinky in 2013. Paul now has six wonderful grandchildren. Paul's activities have included camping, white water canoeing, sailing, golf, and family activities. He retired from Bath Iron Works in 2010. He then joined People Plus where he enjoys the **Write On Writers** and table tennis, along with his golf and family activities. In 2013, he self-published three books; REFLECTIONS, Some Thoughts on Life and Love; A JOURNEY; and IMPRESSIONS From an Ordinary Person of Famous People I've Never Met. In 2014, he self-published *The Sands of Time, Life with and Life After Pinky,* a compilation of 80 pictures, 80 poems, and more than 150 short stories from over 45 years of family life. All books are available on amazon.com/books.

THE HARP

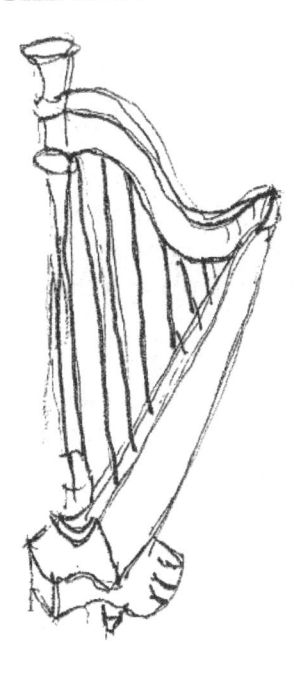

A crowd gathered around the warm campfire
    in the middle of the small country square
To listen to the old story teller
    in the chill of the late evening air.

He sat cross-legged on the plaza,
    bundled in a cloak that covered his head.
His eyes peered into the fire.
    This is what he said.

There's legend that I know of,
    about a harp that's made out of gold.
It lies hidden deep in a forest
    by a stream that runs clear and cold.

It's said this harp is magic
    when the wind plays on its strings,
and those who hear the music,
    can make wishes and get beautiful things.

P.K. Allen

But first, heed this fair warning
    before venturing on that long trip.
Don't touch that harp while it's glowing,
    or a curse will take a death grip.

Now, Billy was a young man about town
    who loved to roam and play
in the forests, mountains, and valleys,
    sometimes all night there he'd stay.

One evening, along about twilight,
    as he strolled on a mountain rim,
he heard a bubbling waterfall,
    and decided to take a cool swim.

Upon nearing the crystal-clear water,
    Billy's eyes beheld a glorious sight.
The most beautiful harp he'd ever seen
    was glowing there in the twilight.

Then the wind began to whisper,
    and the harp began to play.
The night air was filled with music,
    and the trees began to sway.

Billy just stood there gazing
    at the harp in the cool evening dew.
He recalled a story about a legend.
    So, it's true he thought, it's really true.

As he closed his tear-filled eyes
    while making a wish for love,
The music grew louder and louder
    and a chorus joined in from above.

By now the harp was so brilliant,
    just glowing there in the night.
Billy longed to reach out and touch it,
    to feel its soft warmth and pure light.

P.K. Allen

He swam quickly through the cold water,
    and reached up to touch that warm glow,
when a blinding flash suddenly engulfed him.
    About the curse, he did not know.

Did Billy's wish ever get granted,
    or was the curse his unfortunate fate?
I can see by the look on your faces,
    for the answer you sit there and wait.

Well, I really don't know where young Billy went,
    or whatever else happened that day,
but if you'd like to know how to get to the harp,
    I can point you in the right way.

As the old story teller stood slowly and pointed,
    to a place far out in the cold,
everyone there took notice
    of the ....

Before I finish my story
    of a mystery you surely can solve,
take note of the clues I've presented
    for your mind to unfold and resolve.

Take a moment to reflect a bit
    to work it out in your head,
and decide upon your conclusion
    as to whether or not Billy is dead.

    (Pause to reflect)

Now we'll go back to my story,
    to where the climax takes place,
and proceed on to the conclusion,
    to see the surprised look on your face.
Remember,

P.K. Allen

Billy swam through the cold water,
    and reached up to touch that warm glow,
when a blinding flash suddenly engulfed him.
    About the curse, he did not know.

Did Billy's wish ever get granted,
    or was the curse his unfortunate fate?
I can see by the look on your faces,
    for the answer you sit there and wait.

Well, I really don't know where young Billy went,
    or whatever else happened that day,
but if you'd like to know how to get to the harp,
    I can point you in the right way.

As the old story teller stood slowly and pointed,
    to a place far out in the cold,
everyone there took notice
    of the glow from his FINGER OF GOLD.

COUNTRY MUSIC

Country music is more than words
with melodies strummed on an old guitar.
It tells about life, love, and happiness
or wounds that leave a scar.

It can tell a story of love lost
or a life that went astray
Living on the dark side,
or of a brighter day.

It lets the listener experience
the emotions it does impart
About life's pains and pleasures
that's sung straight from the heart

STRANGE PHONE CALLS

Wrong Number

One afternoon years ago, the phone rang. My wife. Pinky answered it, then turned to me and said, "It's for you."

I took the phone from her and said, "Hello."

The caller answered, "Paul, I got the stuff and I have it all divided into nickel bags. How many do you want?

I replied, "This is Paul, but not the right Paul you are looking for. If I were you, I would be more careful dialing."

"Click!"

Afternoon Delight

One afternoon back in the 1980's, the phone rang. My wife Pinky answered it.

"Hello."

"Jane, this is Bill. Put on something sexy because I have the afternoon off and I'm coming home."

Pinky replied, "Bill, I'm sorry to tell you this, but this isn't Jane. You have the wrong number."

Bill seemed completely embarrassed and began apologizing. "I am so sorry; I hope I didn't offend you."

"That's okay Bill, have a GREAT afternoon."

Pinky then hung up the phone. A minute later it rang again.

"Hello."

"Jane, you'll never guess what just happened."

To which Pinky replied, "It just happened again."

P.K. Allen

THE GRASSHOPPER

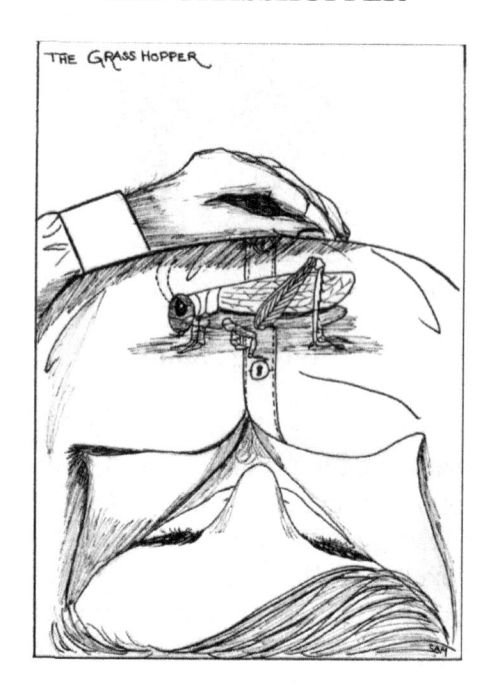

A grasshopper jumped right onto my chest
In order to take a well-deserved rest
From his long journey across the cut grass
Or to avoid danger until it did pass.

He looked down at me, right into my eye,
While flat on my back there I did lie,
Just like he knew he was safe from all harm,
Though I could end that with a flick of my arm.

How nice it would be if we all used that creed
And lent ourselves there in times of need
For other poor souls who from life's path stray
And happen to stumble right in our way.

P.K. Allen

CRAZY LADIES?

We're running late as usual,
she hasn't even begun to dress.
It really makes me crazy
and causes a lot of stress.

Finally, the suit and scarf are on,
but wait, here comes another catch.
When she goes to put her socks on,
she finds that they don't match.

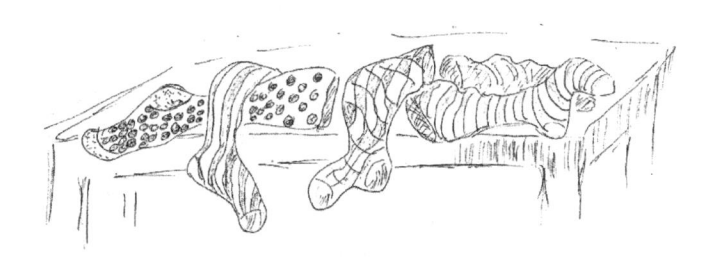

So, we have to start all over
even though they're out of sight,
because she can't go out in public
knowing they're not right.

It's back to the closet again
to find an outfit that's complete,
and matches in style and color
from her head down to her feet

Finally, she's all ready to go,
and we're only thirty minutes late.
Is it just me who's going crazy,
or do other men share the same fate?

P.K. Allen

LOVE AT FIRST SIGHT

Our eyes meet
Joining as one
Each knowing the outcome
Before an embrace has begun

Staring, sharing, caring
Imposing its own will
Our lives passing before us
While time is standing still

MEMORIES FADE

Memories of a lifetime
Stored in the mind
Some easy to open
Others harder to find
Seeing a face
Forgetting the name
The older we get
More of the same

Then comes that day
Which may not be far
When we look in the mirror
And don't know who we are
Bringing sorrow to friends
We've known many years
Having grown up together
And now replacing laughter with tears

P.K. Allen

TWO TALL SHIPS
(for Carol)

We sailed in from different directions,
each leaving from a different shore,
closing the distance between us,
not knowing what was in store.

Each minute we came nearer
we took on a better view
of the beauty of our ages
with differences but a few.

And after sharing some special moments
that brought old feelings back to light,
we went upon our separate ways
like two tall ships passing in the night.

P.K. Allen

THE MEANING OF LIFE?

Wandering thoughts
Between life and death
Make me wonder
What life has meant.

Like a nomad roaming
The dunes of hot sand
Searching for an oasis
In a vast arid land.

Friends I remember
The birth of a life
Death of a daughter
The love of a wife.

Achievements and disappointments
Events along the way
Birthdays and weddings
And funerals some days.

Bringing close together
Those who would share
Their thoughts and emotions
To show that they care.

The smell of a rainstorm
The sense of hearing and sight
Along with tasting and touching
And knowing what's wrong from what's right.

P.K. Allen

A walk on the beach
A ride in the car
The vastness of space
Looking up at the stars.

A God up in heaven
The devil down below
The measure of a lifetime
Tells the direction we'll go.

Leaving me to wonder
What's the meaning of life?
With all of its passageways
Between happiness and strife.

While each day the sun rises
To brighten the sky
Asking that question, but…
The only answer is…Why?

I WRITE

I write for pleasure
And to fill a great need.
I write for fun
And for lessons to heed.

I write about happiness
And about human strife.
I write about love
And about a good life.

I write to make people think
And to make them aware.
I write to make people laugh
And to make them all care.

I write about courage
And what's wrong and what's right.
I write about freedom,
And that's why – I WRITE.

Sally Curtis Hartikka

Sally is a retired librarian with an interest in history, travel, and choral singing. She has published two books. Her first book, *Sing the Lord's Song in a Strange Land*, is the story of Elizabeth Meader Hanson, who was captured by natives in 1724 and taken to Canada along with her children. Her second book, *The Bridge*, was published in 2017 and showcases her recently developed interest in poetry. Her days are filled with singing, writing, and volunteering.

Sally Curtis Hartikka

THE OUTSIDE WORLD

Sophie was getting very bored and angry. She'd been holed up in her room now for three weeks with only a knock on the door when food was left outside. Already greatly irritated that her children had taken away her car and sent her to this senior center, the pandemic was making things much worse. The people running *Cozy at Home* were no longer allowing visitors and had stopped all interaction between residents. She was feeling lonely and neglected, and the four walls were closing in on her. This was a prison, and she hated it. What had she done to deserve this? Yes, she'd had that little fender-bender, but it was nothing, really. It could have happened to anyone. However, Bill and Sandra thought that it gave them the opportunity to take away her Buick, her lifeline to the rest of the world. She could no longer go shopping, attend church or meet her friends for lunch. They next decided she would be happier living in a controlled setting with other people her age. She told them she already had a social life and wouldn't go. However, she had appointed Sandra power of attorney several years ago, and her daughter decided she was no longer competent to take care of herself. Really! She could outwalk all of them, mow the lawn herself, cook her own gourmet meals, and finish the New York Times crossword puzzle every Sunday…in ink! She was in great shape!

From her room on the third floor, Sophie could see a forested area about a mile away, and she yearned to go there. The birds seemed to be beckoning to her, though she could not hear them through her permanently closed windows. A plan began to form in her mind…a plan to escape. She started a list of what she would need to live in the woods. She researched ways to avoid being recaptured, and she began hoarding food…lighter items she could carry in her backpack. She knew she didn't have enough to last very many days, and water would be a problem, but she had a canteen and would worry about that later. The north woods hermit had lasted for years by breaking into cabins and taking food (she couldn't bring herself to use the word "stealing"), so perhaps she could do the same. In any case, she was looking forward to the adventure and to making a statement about the inhumanity of being forced to live in senior housing

Her daughter called her about every other day, her son on the weekends. She decided she would leave at night, early in the week on a day following Sandra's call. Since the staff would probably not check on her until her meals had accumulated for a couple of days, she figured she had about forty-eight hours to travel before she was missed. Thus, she quietly slipped out of her room at two a.m. early on a Tuesday morning. It was near the end of May, so she should not have to worry too much about the cold; in any case, she was dressed in layers so she didn't need to pack a jacket…just a raincoat.

Getting out of the building unseen was a piece of cake. The faint lighting in the hallways was enough to enable her to see, and there was nobody around. She exited through the kitchen via a back door. Outside, she took a breath of the fresh, dewy spring air and exulted in the lift it gave her. She was heady with excitement as she slipped through the deserted streets toward the woods. She took a well-worn path through the trees, her flashlight showing the way. She knew that when daylight came, she would have to leave the path and head deeper into the woods to lessen the chance of being spotted, but for now the going was fairly easy.

She could hear the rustling of small animals and the bubbling of a small brook nearby, but nothing else disturbed her. She was in good shape for a woman her age, and by the time the first birds started warbling she figured she had probably walked about five miles. She had no idea where she was headed and hoped she was going away from civilization, not towards it. At least she heard no signs of traffic. Though not a path, eventually there was a break in the underbrush, and she pushed through it. She came upon a lovely grove of trees where she decided to stop and rest. She placed her raincoat on some moss, sat down for the first time since leaving the center, ate a granola bar and had some sips of water from her canteen. Then she leaned back against a tree and fell asleep.

When she awoke, the sun was high in the sky, and her watch said it was eleven-thirty. She felt exhilarated, and after eating an apple and drinking a few more sips of water, she continued in a direction that lay away from the trail. Her progress was slow but steady, and she took time to enjoy her environment,
noting the different birds and their calls. She felt alive for the first time since Bill had died over four years ago. She walked all

afternoon and began to note that the terrain was changing, and it was becoming hilly. She thought she was heading west or northwest, and that was good. There were apt to be fewer people in that direction. About eight o'clock she finally settled down for the night and figured she was probably far enough away so she wouldn't have to worry about folks looking for her. In any case, they probably wouldn't begin a search until sometime tomorrow.

Sophie covered herself with the light blanket she had managed to pack, slept well, and started the next morning refreshed. There were still no traffic noises, but at one point she thought she heard the sound of a helicopter off in the distance. It didn't come closer, so she stopped worrying and continued her trek, stopping to rest and eat a bit of something every few hours. After a long day of hiking, she settled down for another night in a beautiful spot near a pond. As the evening wore on, she realized her choice for a bed was probably a poor one. The black flies were busy. There were hordes of them, and they were biting. A lot. Drawing blood. She covered herself up as much as possible, but they were in her eyes and nose and getting up her sleeves. Before long she was miserable. She moved away from the water, hoping she could lose them. She couldn't; they had locked onto her scent and followed. She found a good spot, gathered some wood and started a small fire. She was in a quandary, for she knew that it was the smoke that might keep them away, something she could create by putting some evergreen boughs on the flames. If she did that though, she would reveal her location to any aircraft that might be looking for her. She would have to take her chances if she wanted to have any blood left in her veins by morning.

She slept fitfully for the rest of the night ready to put out the fire if she heard anything, but she didn't. At dawn she covered the ashes with dirt and filled her canteen from the pond before moving on. She was tired now…tired and hurting…and itching. The bites had produced big welts all over her skin, and it took a great deal of self-control to keep from scratching. She took a couple of Tylenol, hoping for some relief. She did not make good time this day and towards afternoon she began to feel ill. Her stomach was aching and making strange noises, and she soon learned why as violent diarrhea overtook her. She hadn't known it, but the pond water was spiked with giardia. Had she boiled it, she would have been fine,

but now these parasites were in control of her digestive system, and she was in real trouble. Suddenly she thought she might have made a mistake; perhaps her freedom was not worth this misery. She would go back if she could, but there was no way she could find her way at this point. She decided to stop and make a fire. This time she made no effort to hide the smoke, throwing ever more pine branches on the blaze. The thick smoke helped with the bugs, but nothing could help her stomach distress. She could not eat; she could not sleep. When morning came, she kept feeding the fire, creating more and more smoke, now hoping she would be seen. When she heard the helicopter mid-morning, she waved her arms, then her raincoat, praying the pilot would spot her. He did, and she watched as a hardy individual was lowered to the ground. Then the helicopter hovered
briefly before flying off.

    The rescuer, a woman named Sue, came over to talk to her, then hooked up a saline solution and covered the bites with calamine lotion. There was little else that she could do. Sophie would have to wait for a ground party to carry her to a location where the helicopter could land, then take her to a hospital.

Sally Curtis Hartikka

    For several weeks, she was unable to return to her room at *Cozy at Home*. During that time, she stayed in a wing of the hospital not used for Coronavirus patients. She was badly dehydrated and still couldn't keep anything down. She was allowed no visitors due to restrictions brought on by the virus; however, she did hear from her kids. Boy, did she hear from them! They were furious with her! She tried to explain to them why she had run away and finally got the message across to Sandra. When at last she was released from the hospital, restrictions due to the virus had been eased. As she and her daughter pulled up to the senior center, Sandra walked her over to a little second-hand Beetle in the parking lot and handed her a set of keys. "Here, Mom, I think you've earned this," she said.

THE BLUEBIRD

Little blue bird with a rose-colored tummy,
You've garnered my love and respect.
You're new to my area; I'm glad to meet you,
And I think you're just about perfect.

What brings you to our town this year?
I hope it's not a onetime fling
And you'll continue to reappear
And visit us every single spring.

Sally Curtis Hartikka

RAIN

The rains come
They refresh the parched earth
A drink of life
A chance for rebirth.

The grass turns green
And new plants appear
It's time for renewal;
It's the spring of the year.

There's new hope
And we set out with vigor
To overcome obstacles
With renewed verve and rigor.

A MAINE LAW

It's against the law for Mainers
To step out of a plane while in flight.
It sounds as if the law framers
Think that Mainers are just not too bright.

I've never heard of a Maine native
Attempting this irrational action.
Instead, I think that the lawmakers
Were trying to find a distraction.

Perhaps they were tired of nothing to do
And came up with this regulation
So they would have something to talk about
When they gave their long-winded oration.

Sally Curtis Hartikka

THE YEAR MAINE BURNED

Smoke covered the sky, a blanket
Of woodsy, pine-tinged scent
That drifted from a large brushfire.
The odor sometimes came and went
But was mostly always present.

My mother helped the Red Cross;
Brewed coffee, really strong;
Made sandwiches and doughnuts
To feed the weary, dirty throng.
Firemen found the days so long!

This was the year Maine burned,
Nineteen Forty-Seven the date
When forest fires burned throughout
Our parched, tinder dry, pine tree state.
And winds blew, would not abate.

From Wells and its surrounding towns
To Bar Harbor's millionaire's row
Devastation could be seen.
Houses burning, night skies aglow
And weary men struggling below.

Bowdoin, near Richmond, the fire close by,
The one where Mother's doughnuts fed
The toiling firemen from neighboring towns
Who struggled to create a beachhead
While inhabitants watched the fire with dread.

For two weeks or more, our scenic state bled,
Her forests, her meadows, her houses wiped out.
Thousands homeless, humans and creatures.
All brought on by a months-long drought.
The end finally coming when rain spread throughout.

Sally Curtis Hartikka

THEME PARKS

My favorite theme park's the great outdoors,
'Specially in the State of Maine.
There's so much you can do here
Without having to get on a plane.

Maine has got just everything,
Everything it takes.
Magnificent Atlantic shoreline,
Rivers, ponds and lakes.

We have mountains for climbing,
Beautiful scenery galore.
Lots of hiking and biking
Through shaded woodland floor.

If you're not the active type,
There's still a lot to do:
Plenty of country stores
And lots of rustic views.

We're famous for our lobster,
'Specially stews and rolls.
Gourmet restaurants in the cities
And steaming seafood chowder bowls.

I have no desire to travel away
To other parts of our nation.
I'm happy right where I am
To have a Maine staycation.

Sally Curtis Hartikka

HEROES

What is it that makes a hero?
A person with courage to spare?
What is it that makes a hero?
Who's bravery we'd all like to share?

Who is it that is a hero?
A person who heads into danger
To help someone in trouble
Whether friend or foe or stranger?

Police and fire personnel,
Often at great personal threat,
Spend their careers helping others,
And to them we are all in debt.

But they're not the only examples
Of heroes that we know.
Some people display silent courage
That doesn't always show.

A young child who sticks up for a friend
Who's been bullied for whatever cause
Is certainly being courageous
And deserves a round of applause.

A politician who votes his conscience
Despite what his party commands
Can be really brave and heroic
When he takes a one man stand.

There are many heroes among us
Who act bravely every day
Without having their courage
Be out there on display.

Sally Curtis Hartikka

ZOOM

We gather together to figure out Zoom,
Each from his or her very own room.
Why is my picture not showing on screen?
Am I not there? Am I not seen?

Help everyone, are you able to hear me?
I thought I clicked Zoom…So how can that be?
Wait, I believe that now I have got it.
So let me straighten things out just a bit.

Oops, I think I've lost you again,
Although you still come in now and then.
OK, I think I get it now,
Though something's still not right somehow.

I only see one other person this time.
Where are my other partners in crime?
You say I have to "click gallery" …
Where on earth on the screen would that be?

Now I see you all, and that's fine.
My, it's so nice to all be online.
What, you say our time is now done?
But I just got on; we've just begun!

Elizabeth "Betty" Bavor

Betty was born in Sterling, Massachusetts, where she grew up on a farm and orchard. She earned a BS degree in Physical Education (PE) from Sargent College, Boston University, and a MS in Education from University of Bridgeport in Connecticut. She taught PE in New Canaan, Connecticut for 8 years.

Betty married her husband, Gordon, and became a stay-at-home mom enjoying raising their two children. Her family is rounded out with a stepdaughter and several grand and great-grandchildren. She and Gordon enjoyed years of traveling, camping, and boating on Long Island Sound, along with community events and supporting the interests of their family.

Betty moved to Topsham, Maine, where she continues to enjoy adventures, educational opportunities, making new friends and volunteering. She is grateful for the People Plus organization which has provided numerous learning experiences including honing her writing skills among supportive talented people.

Elizabeth "Betty" Bavor

ALL MY CHILDREN TOGETHER

It was a glorious celebration with all my children together after many years. I met my stepdaughter at the train station, her final leg after traveling cross country. I had not seen her in over ten years. Later on that day my son and his girlfriend arrived from CT with his boat in tow. I felt joy with all three of my children in Maine Vacationland.

Boating was on the agenda for us as we launched at the Androscoggin Greenway boat ramp in Brunswick. We navigated to Bath seeing eagles, sea birds, seals and wonderful Maine landscape. A second boat launch was at Look Out Point where we explored Harpswell before meeting up for a seafood dinner.

Saturday was the surprise of my life. My daughter did not forget my wish to see the puffins. I had written a state Bicentennial piece in 2019 about Atlantic Puffins and said a trip to Rockport to see Puffins was on my bucket list. We were not going on the tour boat loaded with passengers; we were going on my son's boat! We launched at Round Pond and arrived at Eastern Egg Rock where the Atlantic Puffins breed and nest for a few weeks each year on the island's granite boulders. In our open 18' outboard boat, we drifted with the current observing and listening to the puffins and their chicks as they floated all around us and preened on the seaweed covered rocks. The boat engine was silent. The tide was low providing even more visual pleasure.

Elizabeth "Betty" Bavor

My son and daughter worked together navigating our exploration of these islands. We landed on one of the islands to beachcomb and select a rock as a souvenir. We saw seals, porpoise, and sea birds cruising on the calm seas. It was overcast and just perfect weather for our adventure.

We returned to the dock passing intriguing islands, some with beautiful homes and others pure nature, all Maine's pride and joy. Pulling the boat out onto the trailer was easy. The trip back to Topsham included a stop for an ice cream treat. We all cherished this day together.

Our children reconnected, reminisced about growing up and summer camping vacations. Maybe one day their Spokane sister will move back to New England – possibly Maine! I am proud of each one and pray for their health, safety, happiness and continued success.

CUB SCOUT DEN MOTHER

Our first child, a son, began his Boy Scout journey as a Cub Scout. He became a member of this "pack", as it is called. A parent was required to commit support. So, I was chosen to be a Cub Den Mother for a few years before the boys' transition to Webelos Boy Scouts when Dads and older boy scouts became leaders. (Webelos means, "We'll Be Loyal Scouts"). Cub Scouts was for boys age five to eleven. Tiger, Wolf, and Bear Cubs are now part of Cub Scouts, and there are now girl members! That is another story for another time.

I completed the required training and had 8 –10 boys in my Den. Activities ran year-round, along with learning the promise and law of the pack and motto, "Do your best." Lasting friendships, spiritual ideals, character growth, patriotism, and citizenship are the goals. Den mothers hoped to create fun with a variety of crafts, games, service projects, skill building, and learning together.

There were weekly Den meetings, one being with the Pack. I recently spoke with my son to hear what his memories of Cubs were. The Klondike Derby, a winter event where the boys made a sled and spent a day outdoors having fun on a snowy hill, was his first response. Then a pinewood derby where each Cub was given a kit, with a block of balsa wood, wheels, and axels, to make a car to race on a track. They made rockets to send high in the sky. I reminded him of a tree planting service project at the school. There was a bare hillside by the school and some trees were donated by the Arbor Day Foundation to be planted. We did a nice job but did not put flags to mark them and when we checked their growth, discovered the landscapers had mowed them down. What a teachable moment for disappointment.

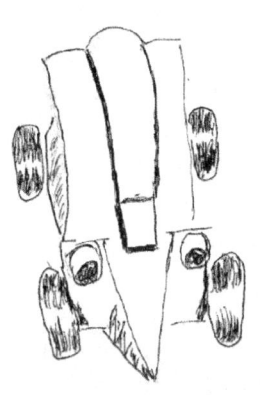

An annual February Blue and Gold dinner celebration with family, recognitions, a speaker, or maybe skits by Dens providing entertainment, was an honor event. The boys transitioned to Webelos and I moved up to Den Leader Coach for a year or so. My son continued his Boy Scouting to the rank of Life Scout, then became a member of the Sea Scouts and had many adventures sailing on Long Island Sound. Some of these Cub Scouts still keep in touch with each other. I know two of them have sons who are Eagle Scouts. My memories of a Cub Scout Den Mother 50 years ago are forever in my heart.

Elizabeth "Betty" Bavor

YES, I AM STILL A GIRL SCOUT

My Girl Scout journey began in 1939 when I became a Brownie Scout in our small Massachusetts country farming town. I was a member of Brownies, Intermediate, and Senior troops from second grade through high school. We learned the Girl Scout Promise. The ten Laws, one for each finger of our hand, guided us to be loyal, kind, cheerful and obedient.

After college, I became a Girl Scout leader in the 1960's taking a troop from Brownies to Senior Scouts. We were part of Connecticut Southwestern Council. I took all the training updating the Girl Scout program and policy. I moved with my troop to new levels and became involved with Neighborhood and Council projects. Girl Scouting troops were arranged by Neighborhood at this time with several troops in each neighborhood. Troops functioned with a patrol system having a patrol leader, scribe, and treasurer. Most Brownie and Junior troops met in classrooms after school. Cadettes and Seniors met in churches, community halls, and some seniors in leader's homes.

Our troop camped year-round, had service projects, celebrated traditional Girl Scout events, sometimes as a troop, sometimes as a neighborhood, and at least once a year as a Council event. Our Troop 705 took many trips promoting the camping and outdoor skills we learned together. The troop's co-leaders were remarkable and cooperative parents who made experiences possible and valuable. When my troop graduated from high school, I became a floating leader helping new leaders and assisting neighborhood programs.

Fast forward to 2015 – I moved to Maine and met Gladys Szabo "a sister scout", also formerly from CT Southwestern Council. I transferred my Lifetime Girl Scout membership to Maine and became attached to Merrymeeting Service Unit Troop 1644 in Brunswick. What a privilege to continue my scouting journey giving back and learning about Maine's scouting events with fine leaders and great Girl Scouts. Thank you, Juliette Gordon

Low – the Girl Scout movement adapts to a changing world. Girls and women believe and make the world a better place living the Promise and Laws of Girl Scouting with unlimited opportunities and adventure. Once a Girl Scout, always a Girl Scout.

THE DAY AT THE LEMON RACE

We had a spur of the moment opportunity to go to a 24-hour Lemon Car Race. My son, with his team, had been driving 2 years in these 24-hour Lemon Car Races. He invited his sister and me to watch at New Hampshire Speedway in Loudon. These races are weekend events starting Friday with learning the track. My son was waiting for us on a bicycle when we arrived at the gate to buy spectator tickets. We followed him to their assigned garage area in the infield pit. He had already driven his morning laps so was able to direct us to a parking space where we could see the cars coming off a hillside curve and proceeding to a straight-away. It was close to their garage area where all the car service activity took place. Crews filled gas tanks to transport to the pit area for refueling and checking their car. They changed drivers in the pit when one had completed their time behind the wheel. It is a restricted area and we watched behind a fence.

There were strict racing rules and regulations which I checked out on the internet for "24 hours of Lemons, the World's craziest race" when I returned home. The motto is, "Racing shouldn't just be for rich idiots. Racing should be for all idiots." Cars could not cost any more than $500 before adding safety required equipment. There were exterior and engine regulations. Drivers also needed to have a pre-competition doctor's physical and required safety clothing before the race. Cars were inspected by officials to assign to classes. The organizers' decision was final to assure the car and driver were safe to participate.

A rule violation penalty could remove the car from the race. Egregious offenses required the driver be secured on the roof with an audio haler and the crew surrounded the car as it traveled the infield and garage areas. The driver on the roof repeated," I am a bad driver. I am sorry," which we witnessed as a crew drove by us, before they are allowed to return to the race. There were other penalties too, called "black flags," calling for time out in penalty box which caused them to lose laps. I hoped it made the race safer.

The race was timed and laps were counted each day. A lap on this track was 1.6 miles. Teams of 4 drivers took turns driving over 100 miles an hour. There were 91 cars in this race that started at 9:30 am and ended at 4:30 pm.

This ending was exciting because my son was the final driver and 40 minutes before the end, he was running out of gas. It was an intense conversation whether to slow down to save gas or make a pit stop. The yellow flag came out which required a slow-down – a blessing. No one can pass. The minutes seemed like hours and he made it to the checkered flag. Everyone was elated. They placed 17th in this final event of the season in their BMW Lemon car. Their weekend drive was approximately 700 miles! They were a great team. All their friends are looking forward to next year.

I had a fun ride around this massive speedway on a quad and could write much more about this glorious day. It is hard to believe my son is so active racing. When he was in high school, he was on a stock car pit crew in Danbury, CT. He was not a driver, parent's decision! I count my blessings having this exciting experience with my children.

UMPIRES – REFEREES – JUDGES – COMMITTEES

The 2020 Summer Olympics are history and umpires, referees, judges, and committees can reflect on decisions they made for athletic performances and many sports' final results. I had the opportunity to be a guest observer on the committee boat for a sail race on Casco Bay. It has been a challenging season for sail racing with storms, no wind, and race cancellations. However, it was perfect yesterday, steady wind, calm sea, and a fleet of 18 Etchells on the starting line. Two races were completed.

Elizabeth "Betty" Bavor

We left the dock in the evening to drop a large inflated mark for the starting line as the "mark" boat took a buoy to the race course turning point a mile or so away. We anchored and waited for every boat to pass by for check in. There was much activity on board prepping for the start of the race.

The first race had a recall as too many boats were over the line early. As we watched them sail away, sumptuous food was set out for dinner and we relaxed. Oh yes, I forgot to tell you, we had a very well behaved and friendly dog aboard named Hazel. The fleet rounded the mark and headed back to the finish line. Every boat received a signal and was recorded when it crossed the line. The course had been shortened due to time limit and a second race was underway without any issues. Clean up time for us came and before long we were blowing the horn and recording winners in the second race. Marks were collected, deflated, and were returned to the dock. Flags, numbers, lines, and race related materials all had their storage location. The committee boat was shipshape in no time. Everyone gathered at the club house where the race committee met to document and record race results. It was social time for the sailors and friends. I enjoyed meeting my daughter's sailing friends. This was a wonderful and unexpected experience.

It had been many years since I was on a committee boat in Connecticut. This club requires boat crews take turns for race committee duty with a professional race leader at the helm communicating, setting the course, calling the times, and directing activity related to flags, information for sailors, starts, and finishes. The Connecticut yacht club's committee boat crew is consistent with retired sailors who still want to be involved, plus extra people as subs.

My husband and I, on our power boat, were chase or stake boat at marks for the season as our daughter sailed on Lightnings and Laser class boats.

I enjoy remembering past adventures and appreciate the opportunity to add more adventures to my memory box by way of a daughter who sails on Casco Bay, Portland, Maine.

Elizabeth "Betty" Bavor

REFRESHED AND RENEWED

I have a question for you. Do you have a time when you felt or feel refreshed and renewed? Everyone has endured an unprecedented difficult year in our lives. Sheltered in place, masks required, normal routines interrupted, food and necessities in short supply, closed business and houses of worship, job loss plus COVID-19 sickness and death forbidding all celebrations and family gatherings which have turned our lives upside down. It is not over as we take one step forward and two steps back with catastrophic social issues, global national crises, storms, floods, fires, volcanoes, and climatic conditions. Often heard, "We are in it together and we will win it!" Have faith, hope, and prayer.

As I ponder this question, I realize that on Wednesday of each week I am refreshed and renewed. The place is People Plus, 35 Union Street, Brunswick, Maine, where magic happens at our *Write On Writers* meeting. These emotions, for me, begin prior to our gathering as each of us creates a story, narrative, poem, memoir, fiction, or nonfiction piece to share around our "family table" of writers. In this moment, as I am writing this piece, I am feeling refreshed in anticipation of reading it out loud and being renewed with joy and fellowship. Our talented members engage with diversity and a wide range of interests. We encourage each other sharing laughs, mystery, empathy and gratitude when we read our published pieces in the monthly People Plus News. We welcome new members to join us and be refreshed and renewed. Thank you People Plus for providing us with this opportunity to be writers and authors.

NEW IN 2022

An unexpected good bye to 2021 and hello to 2022 New Years' celebration for me was when my son and his girlfriend arrived from Connecticut. We all stayed at my daughter's home to watch the Rose Parade and then ventured to Portland's Evergreen Cemetery to see the river otters. I am not sure if this is their common habitat. However, many people lined the banks of a pond to watch these unique animals appear from holes in the ice. Red salmon was thrown on the ice for these playful animals to retrieve.

They then disappeared back in the hole under the ice. Only one was visible at a time. It came quite close to the pond's bank to survey all the visitors with cameras ready. The otter posed for several minutes as if to say, "Here I am for your photo ops! – Happy New Year!"

A second 2022 New Year experience was Geocaching, also known as the World's Largest Treasure Hunt. I remember doing this at a Girl Scout camp many years ago using a compass and topographic survey map. Today, Geocaching is very popular and high tech with people registering on a cell phone or iPad app. Much information leads hikers to sites where a Geocache treasure is hidden. Locations are dotted on the trail app with dates when they were last located, plus a hint or two. We found five on Lisbon and Durham trails plus one at the Lisbon Community Center and another in the community garden. We left a marble in the container at each site as a token if the cache was large enough to hold items. My son and his girlfriend had been participating for a while, submitting details of the container's condition with the date each cache was found or not located. Finders received badges for their success. After our adventures, they were notified they had earned a Maine badge to add to their collection. On their way home they also stopped at L.L. Beans where they found one more hidden by the big boot. If you have not tried Geocaching, check it out – www.geocaching.com. I hope I will have another opportunity to try it again in 2022. It was exciting and fun.

The last joy of 2022 during this family visit was a special dinner to celebrate my soon to be new decade of life. The early celebration was planned including a birthday cake and an evening together playing games. I am filled with gratitude for the gift of 2022. I could not have had a more joyful New Years' weekend. I hope you had family holiday gatherings and I wish everyone a healthy, happy, blessed, and peaceful 2022.

Elizabeth "Betty" Bavor

WONDERS OF THE WORLD – PEOPLE

The Greeks chose the number 7 for the ancient list of wonders because it represents perfection and plenty. Seven was also the number of the five planets anciently known plus the sun and moon. The ancient Wonders of the World were monuments of human achievement using manual labor and crude tools such as Egypt's Great Pyramid, the last standing ancient structure.

Another list of wonders is the classic Great Wonders of the World including more creations by people such as the Great Wall of China, Petro in Jordan, Machu Pichu in Peru, Taj Mahal in India, Christ the Redeemer in Brazil, the Coliseum in Italy, and Stonehenge in England. There are now hundreds of wonders listed throughout the world from antiquity to the present day, including natural wonders, manmade structures, and new discoveries.

I think the true Wonder of the World is People, beginning with Adam and Eve to the babies being born around the world today. Each person's body is similarly designed for movement, intelligence, creativity, knowledge, and efficiency, though each of us is unique in abilities, interests, and appearance. There will never be another person like you which makes each one a "wonder."

I am inspired to recognize people as a Wonder after reflecting on a TV program – "60 Minutes" which reported about the Mars unmanned "helicopter" capable of providing incredible new information. A second presentation was the discovery of an underwater city off Italy's shores which is well preserved and was a place of pleasure for the rich and famous of the time. These events in space and oceans are all possible due to people, so in my heart and mind, we are All Wonders of the World.

Everyone navigates through a changing world. So many new challenging experiences have created personal wonders every day.

Elizabeth "Betty" Bavor

FRIENDSHIP

THERE ARE BIG SHIPS
THERE ARE SMALL SHIPS
BUT THE BEST SHIPS
ARE FRIENDSHIPS [1]

F	Favorite people in your life forever – guardian angels in disguise.
R	Ready to share and play roles in every chapter of each other's lives.
I	Impossible to replace.
E	Eager to bestow unconditional love.
N	Never ever taken for granted or left behind.
D	Determined to support one another in happy and sad times.
S	Smiles and sounds of our voices invigorate the heartstrings.
H	Having good friends to make memories together is a privilege to sing.
I	In the passing of time when friends must be apart, hold those memories cherished in your heart.
P	Pray for your friends who listen and care; call, email, send a note to let them know you are there.

[1] Author unknown

Russ Kinne

Russ has been self-employed nearly all his life. He has worked as a consultant, photographer, writer, boatman, diver, driver, pilot, and even stenographer.

Russ grew up in Rhode Island and went to Brown University when he was 17. When he turned 18, he joined the U.S. Navy serving as an aerial photographer in Pensacola, Florida. Two years later he returned to Brown and earned a degree in Psychology. He then hitchhiked to Alaska and worked for the U.S. Fish and Wildlife Service. He was then master of a 73' racing yawl in the Caribbean for two years. After that, he became a professional photographer-writer and took assignments in 50 states and 65 countries.

Russ has written two hard-covered books, several paperbacks, and numerous columns and stories. His first work of fiction, *Rosie's Lightning*, was published in 2013.

Russ Kinne

ADVICE TO MY YOUNGER SELF

Well, hello, Russ Kinne at age 14! You seem to be in good shape, healthy and apparently sane. You must have picked your parents well. That's a good start anyway.

At my age I've been through a lot, and am still here; must be doing something right. But advice to a 14-year-old? Well, for starters, be honest! – *don't lie, ever*. About little things or big things. Liars always get found out, sooner or later, every time. And when people find out you lied, they'll never completely trust you again. And the word spreads quickly. MUCH better not to lie, even if it means not saying anything. You can't unsay a lie.

Be social! – all your life you'll be dealing with people, and the more you do, the better off you'll be. Join clubs, swim teams, baseball/football teams, debating societies, dancing school, theatrical productions, whatever. There're lots to choose from.

And when you're impressed with some girl, slow down! Hormones be damned, this is no time to rush. And – you'll never believe this – but the girl you're so wild over now will hardly turn your head in 3 or 4 years, believe me. Teen years are no time to make lifetime choices.

Get and keep your body in shape. You don't have to be a knobby muscle-man, but even a slightly muscular body is better than a skinny one. You'll avoid fights, attract more girls, and feel better in general.

You're smart, so I probably don't have to say this, but avoid drugs like the plague! Not even one time to "see what it's like." You don't need to know! Drugs are simply slow suicide, and no one needs that. You will of course have beers with friends, and likely get snockered a few times and have a fierce hangover or two. Remember how these feel, and you'll be more likely to avoid them.

And don't EVER, EVER, EVER show off when you're driving a car. The cemeteries are full of kids that did.

OK, now I'll get off my soapbox. You're smart, and I know you'll be sensible and enjoy a good life. Contribute whatever you can to help your country, mankind and the world; everyone should, but few do.

DRIVE LEFT

We all drive on the right – don't we? Well, maybe not. Many American tourists have been to England, or even closer, Bermuda or Nassau – where they drive on the left. In fact, In Bermuda you cannot drive a car until you've lived there for three months! Great for the car accident rates, and also scooter sales and rentals.

Today about 35% of the people, and 25% of the roads, are under left-drive rules. Countries include the Bahamas, Bermuda, much of the Caribbean and Africa, Japan, Brazil, the UK and Ireland, Australia, New Zealand, Jamaica, the Seychelles, the Caymans, and the US Virgin Islands. Just to complicate things, both the US and Canada, many years ago, drove on the left. As did the Scandinavians. Sweden changed sides in 1967, with a **decrease** in auto accidents! Good for you, Squareheads! When the "Chunnel," the auto-tunnel under the English Channel, was built from France (right-hand) to Britain (left-hand) there were frivolous predictions of a massive pile-up in the middle of the English-channel – which of course never happened; they had separate tubes. Samoa, in the Pacific, gets their cars from Australia, where they are MUCH cheaper – but all left-hand-drive. Samoa had been right-hand-drive for 100 years – but switched back in 2009 to accommodate the vast majority of their vehicles and their drivers. Makes sense.

It all apparently started with horse riders, who held the reins in their left hands, and the whip in their right, since most people are right-handed. It was easier and safer this way. The first major road in the US was the Philadelphia-Lancaster turnpike, and it was made right-hand drive, in 1792.

So, I guess we're stuck with right-hand drive roads in America.

Russ Kinne

ON WRITING

If Stephen King can write a book about writing, I think I can manage a short article which I hope will be of benefit to our little group.

Writing can be a smooth process, a near-impossible task, a rewarding one, and an awfully frustrating one. And a few other things I'm sure I've missed.

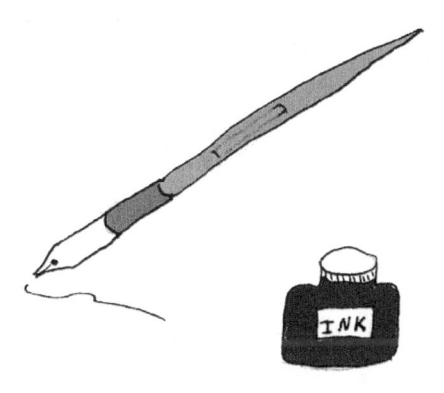

It sounds so simple! – just sit down and put the thoughts in your mind down on paper. And yes, that's all there is of it, BUT – you can't be disturbed while you're writing or it will go SO slowly you may even give up on it.

So that means that spouses, children, neighbors, and pets are forbidden from talking to you or parading through your writing-room. This, of course, causes some dissention, but there's no way to avoid it.

Your chair must be comfortable, but not TOO comfortable! You'll spend a lot of time in it. A very wise man once said "Writing is applying the seat of the pants to the seat of the chair, and keeping it there." I couldn't agree more, but that's hard to do. I toyed with the idea of installing a locking seat-belt, but never did it. However, you must be comfortable, and that includes managing thirst, hunger and a few other things I'm sure I've missed. Keep a bottle of water close at hand and perhaps even some light snacks, but it's better to stay a little hungry, and a little cool, too. Keeps the brain on alert.

Russ Kinne

And you CANNOT be disturbed! – so put away or unplug the phone – you can get messages later – and silence the doorbell too, if you can Of course keep the TV off! A big DO NOT DISTURB sign on the door may work, or it may not, but it's worth a try, but do avoid distractions. Ernest Hemingway, when writing *Snows of Kilimanjaro*, had a big pit dug in his camp, and wrote at a desk in the bottom of it. He couldn't see anything but dirt! – and it helped him a lot. There are just too many fascinating things in Africa to concentrate on much of anything else.

Some people can write well under noisy conditions, but I know I can't. Norman Cousins (Editor of the *Saturday Review of Literature*) used to write on his commuter-train full of people. I asked him how he did it, and he said he simply turned his mental noise-receptors off, and got a couple hours of work done.

Good trick! – I wish I could do that.

Naoma "Nonie" Moody

Nonie's life started in the small mid-west town of Durand, Michigan. She lived on her family's 56-acre dairy farm located three miles from town and graduated from Durand High School. Nonie soon moved to the Washington, D.C. area and worked as a civil service secretary within both the Department of Army and the Department of Energy.

Nonie married Raymond Moody in 1979 and they have one adult daughter. During those years of raising their daughter, Nonie would volunteer at a library and a retirement home doing activities. Upon retiring in 2008, they joined Roving Volunteers in Christ's Service (RVICS), a volunteer service to Christian colleges, schools, and camps.

They retired again in December, 2014 and moved to Maine to be closer to their daughter's family. Joining **Write On Writers**, a group of supportive writers who have fun and learn from one another, was a dream come true.

Naoma "Nonie" Moody

WEDNESDAY AFTERNOON SLED RIDE

There, we were ready to position ourselves on the old-fashioned runner sled. This was going to be exciting and fun. Our grandson, Oliver, was too eager to hop on. "No, you can't ride on the back, you must ride up front and leave room for Grandpa's feet to steer."

It was a year ago that we decided that the grandchildren, ages two and four, were getting bigger and ready to take advantage of our Cathance river bluff in Topsham, Maine, which is in front of our home.

We decided to start searching for sleds to use on our rather steep ridge that flowed down over the neighbor's open back yard. We first answered the ad to a home near Portland for two toboggans. One was rather small for two people, and the larger one for four to fit comfortably. A neighbor had made both in his basement and gave them to another neighbor when he moved from the area. That neighbor decided they were too big and took up space he didn't have. We paid $50 and took both. The smaller toboggan wasn't what we were looking for, but they came as a package. The smaller one without runners could go in circles and never in a straight line. The bigger one had nice ¼-inch runners and ran perfectly, although it was made out of ¾" plywood and was extremely heavy. After being waxed, it flew over the packed snow.

Our property was originally prepared for a large apple orchard. At the back of the land was a rather shallow wide ditch that provided a nice rain runoff for the hay field. This year, with the weather being snow, rain, freezing, snow again, then rain, and freezing, this ditch was filled full of hard ice. I thought one could take a ride down this long icy ditch for an adventure.

In the meantime, knowing that the toboggan would not be the sled to accomplish this interesting endeavor, we decided to haul out the old one-seater flyer sled used for a Christmas decoration. My husband had a two-seater flyer from childhood in good condition in the attic. We cleaned them both up and waxed the runners and were now in business.

The slope running downhill in the ditch was not steep enough to keep us going even on the ice, so we took the flyer sleds back to the house and decided to take a run on the steeper hill. Grandpa tried out the sled first to make sure everything went smoothly. To our surprise it went very smoothly. He went down over the hill making a wide left-hand curve in the lower part of the neighbor's back yard caught up with the frozen ditch that meandered off towards the woods approximately a quarter of a mile from the house. He never stopped, but with his feet was able to guide the direction of the sled. Oliver took off running after grandpa and caught up with him. I took the little flyer down. Although going a little too fast for me, I made the same curve and catching the frozen ditch. I only stopped once when I got off the frozen ditch and scooted back on and proceeded to the woods. At the beginning of the woods, I put out my boots to stop. What a tremendous ride it was and probably the last, knowing that the next day's temperature would hit 50 degrees and the ice would be melting.

Dusk was starting to set in, but before we put the sleds away for the evening, Ray set Oliver on the sled in front of him for one last ride and away they went. I stayed behind videotaping most of the ride until the apple trees ended my view. After they were back in the kitchen, I asked Oliver some questions. What he said was surprising. "We hit a tree." Well, it was only a little sapling and they were coasting to a stop. What fun we all had and we hoped for more snow and more sledding before the arrival of spring.

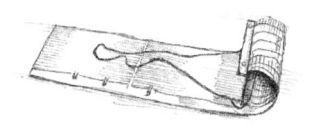

SLEDDING
Haiku

Grandchildren love sleds
Snowing, raining, and freezing
Hot chocolate mugs

Naoma "Nonie" Moody

MOM'S TIN CAN FOOTSTOOL

My parents had little to nothing
So, they patched, repaired, and made due.
This was how they lived in the 1950's
Getting along with few things new.

Mom never wasted a thing
For she was a thrifty person
Rescuing many useful items
Some being helpful, some fun.

It was Dad's empty coffee cans
That were saved and began to stack up.
All she needed was seven of them
To make her little footstool shape-up.

Coffee cans were stripped of their paper
Placing seven cans in a circle design
Topped with soft layered batting
Fastened with rope and tape outline.

The little footstool took form
And an old rug covered tightly.
Mom's vintage footstool was used daily,
And the coffee cans rattle slightly.

Naoma "Nonie" Moody

FOOTSTOOL
Haiku

The vintage footstool
Is carried from room to room
Worth sixty dollars

I'D RATHER SIT

It's a pleasure to sit on the porch
In the big heavy oak rocker
And look over the neighbor's farm
As the breezes sway the field of clover.

It's a pleasure to sit on the porch
Looking at the patio flower bed
As the blossoms are rich in color
And a detected scent is gently spread.

It is a pleasure to sit on the porch
With camera watching and waiting
For that picture of a humming bird
Or a finch at dried zinnia seeds eating.

It is a pleasure to sit on the porch
On a relaxing Sunday afternoon
Watching the many fluffy clouds
Listening to the chirp of a bird's tune.

Naoma "Nonie" Moody

DIAMANTE/DIAMOND POEMS

Writing
Shortest, Longest
Announcing, Corresponding, Notifying
Story, Manuscript, Document, Cookbook
Teaching, Explaining, Recording
Helpful, Humorous
Script

Words
Good, Special
Inspiring, Helping, Refreshing
Bible, Dictionary, Medicine, History
Promising, Captivating, Encouraging
Creative, Simple
Message

Hiding
Fast, Quick
Sheltering, Burying, Disguising
Camouflage, cover-up, outside, voice
Disclosing, Opening, Telling
Happy, Joyful
Siblings

Naoma "Nonie" Moody

WHY I WRITE

Inspiring to write comes from home
Where pencil and paper were available.
Mother like grandmother both wrote
Mostly poetry and some in a journal.

There is adventure in each piece
That has its birth through my feelings
With plain talk and writing truthfully
Whether it be somber or amusing.

Writing is a thrill with fun and pleasure
With each text or rhyme seen in print
A gratification of success with joy
Of a voice that has my fingerprint.

CONDOLENCE

It hit us hard in the middle of March 2020
Just when the new decade was underway.
Life was going well, not many problems
Suddenly our country was placed on delay.

They called the new virus COVID-19
Included a new world-wide pandemic.
Many were dying mostly the very weak
Then Cousin Joey Diegel, 45, parents devastated.

Added to our days were protection masks
And many months later vaccines to guard.
Pandemic statistics were coming down
But Cousin Timothy Akers, 42, parents took hard.

Of the many thousands that have passed
The pain and tears have been expressed.
We honor their lives with living memories
That breathe in our hearts realizing we were blessed.

Naoma "Nonie" Moody

HIDE-AND-SEEK

Summer is gone, but the fun still lingers on in my memory. We have been playing outside among the apple trees. It is hide-and-seek with grandparents and the little ones (three and five) who can only count to about 10. Their hiding is quite unique. If their eyes are hidden so is everything else. The places we hide are out in the open behind trees, a large upright rock, a bush, a rocker, etc.

With fall, the weather has changed and sometimes rains. Then the hide-and-seek moves inside. The five-year-old started school and we now only take the 3-year-old. Hiding is a challenge for the adults, but it is amazing how many places one can hide, especially if you are only three. This little one can hide and not say a word while lying flat under the quilt folded at the end of the bed or crouched between the TV and a couch, under the bed, and still better, inside a closet.

During a trip to the attic with Lily, she sees a small box and wants to look inside. It is stuffed full of brand-new cards of buttons, and she wants to open them all. I show her a plastic bag full of old buttons and tell her she could select one. She chooses the biggest one which is a coat button probably from a woman's old winter coat. It's at least 1 ½ inches across with a raised triangle on the front, a rather ugly button in tan color. Lily takes the button with her enjoying her new found toy. She stands in the middle of the room and says to me, "Grandma, let's hide the button. "You go first for two times, holding up two fingers, and then I'll go two times." We play hide-and-seek with that button for over an hour, and it is so much fun. We could not find the button once, but I eventually found it. I am the guilty one who put it on top of the DVD player right in plain sight.

It is time for lunch, and Lily is washing her button so we have to hurry her up. A couple hours later and in the bathroom, I hear water again. I go and see that the button is submerged in a big bowl of water with lots of suds. I bend over and ask what she is doing, and all I get is a big grin. We examine the button. It does look super clean. I tell her that she has five more minutes to clean her button then she must stop. From the living room I call to Lily that her five minutes are up and to come – and she does.

TIME FOR EVERYTHING

There is appointed time for everything:
A time for plowing, a time for sowing,
A time for sprouting, a time for harvest,
Definite seasons with special timing,

A time to tear down, a time to build up,
A time in history and a time to come.
Occasionally the time is very long.
A hundred times can leave us numb.

There is night time for sleeping time
Which is the proper time since ancient time.
Spending extra time could be a loss of time.
Present time the right time and always prime.

Difficult times may be wilderness times
But in due time, this time is completed.
Since that time a new beginning of time
Spending time until the fullness is perfected.

There is time to give birth and a time to heal,
A time to die but that time we know not.
Making the most of our time at all times
Giving thanks often are times to be sought.

Virginia (Ginny) Sabin

Ginny is a native Mainer born in Portland. She attended local schools, graduating from Deering High School. She wanted to major in English, but that didn't happen. Instead, she went on to Massachusetts General Hospital School of Nursing, U.S. Navy Nurse Corps, Columbia Teachers College, and many years later to Boston University for an MS Degree in Mental Health Nursing. For twenty years before retiring she worked as a psychiatric nurse clinician. She raised a daughter and a son and now is enjoying four teen-aged grandchildren.

At age forty, she began to write poems, drawing inspiration from her love of family, her work, and living in the Harpswell pines for the past 35 years. Her poems blend resonating moods of the human condition with lessons learned from her garden.

Virginia (Ginny) Sabin

THE SEA SO WIDE

My boat so small
A stray barrel, bobbing aimlessly.

The men not in the least in awe…not noticing,
drinking coffee, laying new traps,
pulling traps from yesterday's catch,
gutting, cutting, scraping,
cleaning and dressing for market.

Going home
Tasting ocean
Covered with blood, guts, and glitter. *

Virginia (Ginny) Sabin

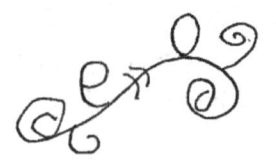

LIFE MEANINGS

Becoming possible
Possible what?
Just possible.
No being without existence
A lifetime waiting
As I fritter away time and mettle
To satisfy and not leave drying
A thirst for sounds rhythmical and metrical
While aging, as I am, in time finite,
Truth and beauty are mined in ageless lines
And still excavated from that same site.
A golden and brilliant light it finds.
What pure metal to explore at any age.
Telling metaphors in many layers,
Freedom of words on a metered page,
Tedium, or ti tum, tum ti for flairs
It is a beginning and not an end.
What time, what other time, is there to mend. *

Virginia (Ginny) Sabin

GARDEN OF WEEDEN

A garden conceived many years ago
Ambitious and daring
Defying possibility in a forest primeval
Mirrors my mood

The fallen trees, the felled trees

A chipmunk, a vanishing blip
A puzzled and patient cat waits

A perennial parade of beauty
Dead headed, beheaded

An overhead of Navy planes
Too close to my island of toil and tranquility
"No man is an Island,,,."

My drive for Eden so strong at dawn
Dwindles in the heat of midday
Recharges daily
In the race to remove tough weeds
And cover the earth with mulch *

COMES AND GOES

Spring arrives so abruptly
Or so it seems
Why only yesterday morning
Frost spread its glitter
Over bare trees, brown grass
And bulbs at the starting gate
Frost leaves so abruptly
As magically as Spring on arriving
Forsythia will
Flaunt its wild sprays of brightness
In darkened woods *

Virginia (Ginny) Sabin

SPRING IS HERE

Pussy willow bud
Waits on a twig
Braving the lion's roar

Under snow crocus bloom
Poppy's green fern show
Primrose grace gentle slopes
Of sturdy pine and oak

Dormant bulbs boldly thrust
Drifts of daffodils
In a brown landscape

And winter is gone

LIFE IS GOOD

My life is good, sunflowers growing on trees
A torrent, a trickle, a stream
A river of tears, of fears
Music
Filling an ocean of wound
A torrent of words
In a poem that is me

Virginia (Ginny) Sabin

CHRISTMAS TREE

Evergreen
In winter
Starlit
In snowdrift
Branches
Snow covered and icy
Winterberry and holly adorn
Boughs heavy with fir
An empty nest, a robin's nest
A diamond studded snow covering all
Wait another spring

A GARDEN

Walking alone and old
In a garden of memory
A garden having hours, days
So precious
Who knows
A year

A year
Of falling leaves
First snowfall
Another Spring
Pushing up
Who knows *

Virginia (Ginny) Sabin

MAKE BELIEVE SKY

It is different now, this room
It's a make-believe sky of pink and blue
Tiered with elaborate balconies
Its classic cream and gold columns
And mirrors reflecting then and now

Then was a ball for graduating nurses
A borrowed gown, a borrowed beau
Knowing the first and last dance
Encapsulated all the magical time we had
Under that make-believe sky

Now decades later
The mirrors, molding, and painted sky
Had withstood time
The dance floor was carpeted
To muffle the sound of a throng of professionals
In their cerebral song and dance of geriatric psychiatry *

I lean backwards and look up
That make-believe sky fills my eyes
And I wonder the value of knowing
When it's the end

Slipping from shore In darkness
Waking to infinite sky meeting infinite ocean

* Previously published in *Bloomings Of Mind, Body, Spirit* by Virginia Sabin © December 2020

W.A. Mogk

Wayne lives in Topsham with his artist/author wife, Marsha, and their nine wonderful cats. They moved to Maine in 2006 after spending almost two decades in New Mexico where they experienced new adventures and learned about the southwestern culture.

Wayne grew up in New Jersey. He enjoyed reading science fiction, gravitating towards authors like Bradbury, Wells, Asimov, and others. They are a definite influence on his own writings today.

Wayne has traveled across the United States by car, van, and motorcycle. He notes that each part of our country has something unique to offer, as do the people who live there. This traveling "bug" took him to Wisconsin, Idaho, Colorado, Utah, Texas, Arizona, New Mexico, California, and other places.

All these adventures add to the treasure chest of memories and facts that Wayne draws upon for his stories that he hopes people will find intriguing and entertaining.

W.A. Mogk

WHERE THERE'S SMOKE...

    The alarms went off all over town, indicating smoke from a nearby forest fire. The residents of Flagstaff, Arizona, had hoped this day would never come, but with a changing climate, and sustained drought, it was not that surprising.

    Surveillance aircraft were sent out to spot the fire and give first-responders accurate information so they could form a plan of action. When the reports came in, they indicated flames could not be seen anywhere, and places that the smoke had drifted away from showed no burning whatsoever. It was as if nothing had happened. These mysterious findings were reported every time the smoke was encountered: no flames, no burning, no destruction.

    Then news reports started mentioning other places around the country where similar situations had occurred; lots of smoke, but no fire. Even more curious, reports of strange smoke were recorded drifting over cities and towns far away from any forests. No one knew what to make of it.

    Eventually the plumes of smoke dissipated, leaving people and scientists scratching their heads as to what had happened. Months passed and slowly but surely, the whole episode faded in the public consciousness and was stored away in the recesses of the brain where unimportant things dwell in solitude.

    Then a similar phenomenon began happening in Europe. Anticipating a recurrence somewhere else on earth, scientists in the US dispatched a research team to one of the locations. They quickly set up a base of operations, then sent in a drone aircraft to record images and gather data. On one such pass through the cloud of smoke, the drone collided with something and was knocked out of commission. When the wreckage was found, everyone's jaw dropped. There it was. A craft obviously not made by human hands and just as obviously, built to carry people or something like people.

W.A. Mogk

The alien vessel had nosedived into the ground, scattering pieces along the side of a hill. The largest of these looked fairly intact and was surmised to contain the craft's occupants. After prying open a hatch-like section, a member of the research team entered. There were several human shaped forms piled on top of one another in a heap, apparently jammed together in a pile when their craft struck the ground. All appeared to be lifeless. Then the team member saw the arm of the one on top of the pile move slightly—he or she was still alive!

The creature was removed, still wearing its uniform and helmet, then gingerly transported to a secure medical facility. Others stayed behind to try to discern to what they could about the purpose of the craft and the beings who had piloted it.

The medical team quickly discovered that their patient possessed similar human attributes such as bone structure and organs, and breathed air not much different than our own. The doctors were discussing what treatments to proceed with when they heard – I...speak...your...language.

The startled group turned to stare confoundedly at the form occupying the bed. "I'm in a lot of pain! Can you give me something?"

"You may have a bad reaction to our medicines," said one. "I am enough like you that it will be okay," came the response. A pain killer was administered, and soon the injured survivor from the crash was feeling better, but still needing surgery if it was going to recover.

"What is your name?"

"You can call me Clark."

W.A. Mogk

"Clark, why were you in the cloud?" Clark explained that "his people" had been observing Earth and its inhabitants for many centuries and watched as the environment became degraded to the point of ecological disaster. He and others had come to cleanse the planet to make it viable again. The clouds of so-called "smoke" contained microbes that would aid in restoring the Earth's biodiversity.

"I find that hard to believe, Clark!" blurted out a person standing in the back of the room. Colonel Reed stepped over to Clark's bedside and continued. "I don't think you are here to help us at all! That so-called smoke is probably a biological weapon that's going to kill us all off, so your race can take over our planet. You're here to wage war on us!"

"We are a peaceful race," responded Clark. "We learned long ago not to kill – not each other, nor any other life forms that we encounter. We don't even kill lesser beings for food, as you do, with what you call "meat." That is abhorrent to us. Our diet is entirely plant-based. So, we could not possibly wage war with you. That is not who we are. We are civilized!"

"So far we haven't identified any harmful effects from your cloud," countered Reed, "but when we do, your race will feel the wrath of humanity. Till then, you will remain in custody here in the hospital where you will be treated humanely because that is our way. Doctors, take care of our patients!" Then Colonel Reed turned and left.

That night, a different kind of cloud descended over the hospital and the surrounding area, causing everything within it to lose consciousness. Clark (not his real name) was borne away by his fellow comrades and transported to the far side of the Moon where his people had their staging area and where he received the necessary medical attention.

When "Clark" had recovered enough, he was asked about his experience. "I was completely honest with the Humans and told them we were cleansing the environment. One of their kind thought we were hostile, so I tried to allay his fears by mentioning our respect for life, and non-violent nature. He still insisted that we had come to attack his planet."

"On every world we have tried to cleanse, the inhabitants always jump to that same conclusion," reminded Bortan. "It's a pity they can't think of us as civilized. Civilized beings don't wage war on others."

"Are we still on track to complete the cleansing in about three cycles?" queried Kleek (a.k.a. Clark).

"All indications suggest that our clouds are doing what was intended," affirmed Bortan. "Only now, the Humans are beginning to realize that female pregnancy rates are plummeting. They don't suspect that their race is becoming sterile. Offspring that were in the womb and not affected during cycle one will be sterilized in cycle two at the appropriate time. After that, one more cycle for good measure should guarantee the extinction of their kind. You know what I always say, "If they stop reproducing, it's ours for the choosing!"

"You're so funny, Bortan."

"I know."

PONDERING

He sat on a rock and wondered
what there might be, out yonder.
He looked, thought and pondered;
all kinds of things he conjured.

Vast lands where people dwell;
odd beasts, and riches as well.
Lands full of milk and honey.
No cares, and skies always sunny.

On a rock, still wondering;
dark clouds began thundering.
He rose up, heading for cover,
and forgot about all the other!

W.A. Mogk

SOMEDAY

The first snowfall came unexpectedly. They had been telling us for years and years that someday it would happen. All that was needed was enough moisture in the atmosphere and it would snow...someday!

Our parents had told us that Great-Great-Grand Daddy had known snow and rain. It's really hard for me to imagine rain. It needs to be much warmer for that to happen. But snow! It's cold enough to snow!

Daddy looked up some facts and says when it snows just a little, it's called a "dusting." If it snows a lot and it's windy, it's called a "blizzard." People can get lost in blizzards and might not be found for days. That's really scary! I don't like getting lost at any time.

Great-Great-Grand Daddy came here with the first settlers. I was told that they were brave pioneers who wanted a challenge, and who were going to create a new future from the ground up. It would take a long time, longer than a single lifetime. So, each pioneer was given a large tract of land that they could pass down to their descendants, which they could use to create revenue and support themselves.

That's where we live now, on the property Great-Great-Grand Daddy picked out for himself. A huge area that also goes right up the mountain. I think owning a mountain is stupid because it's nothing but rocks. Daddy says, "it has potential." I guess potential means you can do something with it.

Daddy says that when snowfall becomes a common occurrence, that he and other relatives are going to open up a ski resort; it's what Great-Great-Grand Daddy had envisioned (talk about planning ahead!). Daddy says that as more moisture gets pumped into the Martian atmosphere, it just has to snow more, and that will be good for the ski business. I could even be a ski instructor!

I don't really know if sliding down a hill dodging rocks is for me, even though Daddy says they would make it safe.

Here on Mars, we Martians can't do all the things that our distant cousins on Earth can do, but we're making progress. Some day we might even be able to swim outside. Now wouldn't that be something?

W.A. Mogk

AT THE BOTTOM

The heat is almost unbearable. You have breathed rarified air all day and into the night. Now you lie in the darkness on a slab of rock for a bed, looking skyward. Periodically, you cast your hand into the trickle of water that meanders slowly down towards the Colorado River; the destination that you could not reach. Salvation was too far and out of grasp, though it looked just a stone's throw away. The anticipation of cool liquid relief faded into an unattainable dream.

In a half daze of wakefulness, you keep expecting the heat to dissipate, replaced by a more temperate cloak, but the afterglow of Mother Nature's blast furnace lingers on. You want to sleep, but the wished-for escape into unconsciousness eludes you, even though you are exhausted.

Again and again, you dip your hand into the tepid water, elevating a handful of drops to sprinkle on your chest in a futile attempt to gain a few seconds of coolness. Time is lost to you with <u>now</u> seeming an eternity. The end of eternity can't come soon enough!

Tomorrow when you rise, Arizona's giant pit and canyon walls will imprison you for two more days before narrow, dusty trails lead to a way out. Till then, your endurance will be tested, along with patience and sanity. Surely, hiking across the Tonto Plateau in summer is akin to insanity. The eventual daylight will reveal the barren emptiness you volunteered for, not realizing what was in store. Youth thinks it is immortal, and you are putting that to the test. To fail means to be tested no more. At long last, a tinge of wispy air caresses your face announcing a slight drop in temperature. Then, you see the sun rise!

W.A. Mogk

LABOR RELATIONS

All through the summer there had been unrest in Santa's workshop. By reading newspapers, such as the *Wall Street Journal*, the elves knew that there was a wider world out there with opportunities and better incomes. They had always suspected they were underpaid because Santa paid them under the table. The meager pay was bad enough, but being required to parade under a table and reach up for their checks was humiliating. Things had been different in the past.

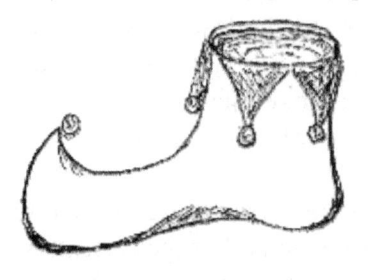

The elves were descended from children that Santa rescued from the sweat shops of Britain in the 1800s. He gave them clothes, good food, and accommodations. In return, the children were more than happy to make toys for Christmas. What they didn't know was that magnets had been sewn into their garments, and after a few generations, the downward pull of the magnetic North Pole caused their offspring to remain tiny. Once the effect was permanent, the magnets were removed and used to make refrigerator stickons. "Waste not, want not," was Santa's motto.

Santa was aware of the discontent among his height-challenged employees and tried to meet their demands halfway. He started a retirement plan, increased medical benefits, and no longer required them to walk under the table. Even so, grumbling persisted, causing Santa much concern.

W.A. Mogk

One day, the Elves were putting the finishing touches on a very large, very ornate steeple bell that had been special ordered and taken weeks to create. In another part of the workroom, a careless elf had dropped a lit cigar into a can of paint thinner, then knocked it over, spreading flaming liquid across the floor. Another elf, the smallest one with the biggest voice yelled, "Let's get the bell outta here!"

Santa was nearby, but mistakenly heard a different word than "bell." He thought the Elves were making a break for it! Santa ran towards the commotion, wondering how he could stop a herd of stampeding Elves. This had never happened before so there were no contingency plans. He arrived at the scene as a dozen coughing workers dragged and pulled the bell to safety. It's no small feat to move a one-ton bell when you have small feet. Santa was grateful beyond belief. If the bell had been ruined or missed its delivery date, he would have to give back his commission which had already been spent to pay gambling debts. (If only that little ball had stopped on 23 red!)

"You boys saved my butt," Santa told them. "What can I do for you?"

"Well, Santa," pronounced a still coughing quality control manager. "We need some changes around here, like better pay and more time off and a new breakroom with an eggnog dispenser, free candy canes, and chocolates anytime. Also, how about hiring a Grounds Keeper to clean up all that reindeer poop? Rudolph may be able to find his way in a fog, but he sure can't find the toilet!"

"I agree to your terms," responded Santa. He knew they weren't asking for too much. Besides, with all the extra sugar they'd be eating, he'd probably get more work out of them anyway!

W.A. Mogk

THE SHADOW

Carl had never been in this part of the building before. It was scary! He had been inching his way down the corridor ever so slowly, not knowing what lay ahead. As he rounded a corner, he thought he saw something—a shadow? Whose shadow?

Not wanting to find out, Carl moved a little more quickly down the hallway. He needed to stay ahead of his pursuer; otherwise, all would be lost. He would never escape!

The way ahead was illuminated by a single lightbulb on the wall. There were two doors nearby, and as Carl approached, he saw it again—the shadow. His antagonist had caught up to him!

Panicked, Carl rammed his shoulder into one of the doors, only to be greeted with pain and disappointment. He threw himself at the other and it gave way, his momentum carrying him far inside. Quickly finding a light switch, he discovered that he was in a kitchen; just the place to grab a knife and defend himself. He thought he heard footsteps. He prepared to meet his unseen foe as sweat beaded on his forehead. Then, the door slowly opened, and a voice said, "Easy Carl—you're safe now."

Later, an attendant asked, "Why do you think Carl left his room?" "Beats me," came the reply. "Usually, he's afraid of his own shadow!"

IT'S UNIVERSAL

    Their meeting was unexpected, actually startling. To suddenly turn and see two giant eyes looking your way can be unnerving. Now, however, Edmund had grown accustomed to the features of his new companion, so he hardly gave them a second thought.
    Edmund had been in a clearing, and completely exposed, when he saw what appeared to be a dangerous creature. After all, Tia (her name, he found out later) had a face similar to cats back on Earth. Only she was much bigger—human size—and stood upright as well. Edmund had braced himself for an attack from this menacing form, but none came, just long moments of staring. Finally, Tia cautiously emerged from among the trees and walked towards Edmund with arms outstretched in a gesture of peace. Ever since that day, Edmund and Tia had scarcely left each other's side.
    With hand motions, and later, some verbalizations, Tia educated Edmund about what was safe to eat and drink in this new environment. Left on his own, he might not have survived for long. A strange planet with exotic vegetation was no place to find himself marooned. One wrong step could lead to ingesting something poisonous. Edmund was lucky that he had met Tia.
    One day, Tia took Edmund to an area they had never been to before. Looking around, Edmund recognized it for what it was: a crash site! Here was the wreckage of an obvious spacecraft. Tia indicated that that was how she had arrived on the planet. After a brief stay, Tia took him by the hand and lead him to another spot where he saw three mounds of rocks piled in a row. Edmund did not have to be told that they were grave markers. Tia bowed her head as a tear began running down her cheek. Edmund moved his arm and drew her closer to his side, offering what comfort he could to sooth her sorrow. Tia grasped Edmund's other hand and squeezed it tight. In that moment, love and understanding stretched between two worlds and across the galaxy. Two different beings, orphaned together on a strange planet, found that tenderness and warmth were universal traits no matter where one comes from.

Lucy Holm Derbyshire

Lucy grew up in Illinois in a ghetto neighborhood. As a fifteen-year-old, she never had a clue as to what her lifetime career should be. Yet her father, John Frederick Stoll, told her she needed to pick it early. He said she needed to plan ahead even though she was only a sophomore at a Christian boarding high school in Potomac, IL.

Lucy started in nursing at age 17 at Mennonite School of Nursing in Bloomington, Illinois, but she and nine other students had to leave because there were not enough teachers. She believed God had called her into nursing, so she stuck with the profession and graduated from Olivet Nazarene College in 1975 with a BSN.

Lucy practiced nursing in Peoria, IL, from 1975 to 1985, mainly in neurosurgical nursing at St. Francis Hospital and then in Houston, TX, from 1985 to 1995 mainly at York Plaza Hospital and Parkway Hospital. Back in Illinois again, she worked at nursing homes from 1995 until 2005 when she moved to Brunswick, Maine, for an RN position in Parkview Hospital.

She recently joined the **Write On Writers** and enjoys writing and sharing her life experiences with others.

Lucy Holm Derbyshire

THE RABBIT

My biology teacher at Wescove High School was Miss Walters. She was from Maine and loved the great outdoors. She was so enthusiastic and happy. She was everyone's favorite teacher.

I was very excited when Miss Walters announced a "pet show." Only animals from outdoors were allowed. No hamsters, gerbils, cats, or dogs were to be brought to class on the day of the show. I was determined to win first prize, but was having problems with keeping my wild pets alive?

Mr. Whipple, my cousin, trapped a wild rabbit and built a lovely wire cage for it. He was trying to help me win first prize. Rabbit could see the surroundings. I kept him in the storage room at the end of the hall in the girls' dorm.

Every morning and evening I fed Rabbit. There were fresh veggies, carrots, cabbage, lettuce, and tomatoes. After three days of the veggies sitting in the cage, I trashed them. Rabbit would not eat or drink and was unhappy in captivity. In a few weeks Rabbit died. He could not be entered in the pet show.

Not to worry. I had an Uncle Emil who did taxidermy and knew I could do it too. I stuffed Rabbit with sawdust to show my future children and grandchildren. I saved the bones and cooked them and then wired them together like the dinosaurs in Chicago's museums.

I put the bones into a large beaker over the giant Bunsen burner in the basement Chemistry lab. While I was practicing for a cantata upstairs in the auditorium, the choir director asked, "Does anyone smell smoke? I smell something burning." It was then that I remembered the rabbit bones. All that was left in the large beaker were gray and black ashes from the rabbit bones.

I learned three things from the Rabbit. Rabbits do not eat while in captivity, taxidermy is fun, and rabbit bones should not be left unattended over a large Bunsen burner.

Lucy Holm Derbyshire

MAPLE SYRUP

Making homemade maple syrup for pancakes is easy. Mix water, sugar, maple extract, and vanilla extract and boil in a medium-sized saucepan over a medium high heat, then reduce heat. Let simmer 3-5 minutes. Yes, I thought that would be easy.

On April 1, 1965 at Christian boarding high school (Wescove High School) in Potomac, Illinois, Miss Loving, the girls' dorm matron, was teaching her five girls an important lesson. "The way to a man's heart is through his stomach." Every one of her five girls, Katie, Barbetta (Lucy's sister), Pat, June, and I were getting turns to cook breakfasts. Today was my turn.

Lucy's graduation picture

Miss Loving had chosen my menu. Pancakes and maple syrup would be available, and if they were not edible, there was a nice selection of cold cereals to substitute.

I had made pancakes at an early age for my father. He liked them thin and the size of the entire cast iron frying pan. The high school gals wanted them thick and the size of cup saucers.

When I had the pancakes ready, the maple syrup in creamers to pour on the pancakes, and fresh milk with blue food-coloring as an April Fools' joke in steel pitchers, I rang a loud bell. Miss Loving and four gals came and sat at the long narrow wooden dining room table. The dining room was quite small but one door connecting it to a large kitchen made it seem bigger.

June sat at one end of the table and I sat at the other end. June had three or four pancakes and put plenty of maple syrup on them. She was the first one to have problems. There were strings of maple syrup dangling from her mouth. She looked as if she was growing a beard suddenly. Next her teeth stuck together because the maple syrup had changed into a glue-like substance. Her fingers stuck to pancakes, fork, and each other. Everything she touched was sticking to her fingers.

The final blow was that June's pancakes became uncuttable. The maple syrup had turned into glass lying across the top of them. No one could cut them, even with the butcher knives I brought from the kitchen.

All pancakes were removed from the dining room and everyone reached for the cold cereal. June was the first one to pour fresh milk on her cereal. She exclaimed, "The milk is blue."
I said, "April Fool." No one thought of it as an April Fools. Not even me. Miss Loving asked for some hot water and had instant coffee as did all the other five gals at the table.

Miss Loving never let her gals cook again after that breakfast. I found out years later that the reason for the strange syrup was that I boiled everything for longer than five minutes. I boiled it for fifteen. Miss Loving's gals had to find other ways to their men's hearts than through their stomachs.

THE SNAKE

I loved snakes. Mr. Whipple caught me a beautiful two-foot pine snake. The snake was kept in a large narrow wooden barrel in the storage room at the end of the girls' dorm.

Lucy Holm Derbyshire

Miss Loving, 28, was the girls' dorm matron, and did not like the idea of a snake living with her five girls in their dorm. I was asked to move the snake to the boys' dorm across the Potomac to the "Ole Judy School." The boys lived on the third floor. High school classes were on the first and second floors. The snake ended up living in the biology lab on the second floor. Mr. West, the boys' dorm-master did not want it either.

Wayne and David, both 13, were the two youngest boys in the high school. They were especially happy to feed Snake. He ate so well that he and became obese. Snake had a diet of fresh frogs, minnows, and bugs, and even enjoyed chicken and other meat scraps. Snake was carefully put back into the barrel with a large brick on top. Sometimes the boys scared all the high school gals except me by dangling it in front of them. One day, Snake escaped. Oh, my goodness. Where was Snake?

Mr. Cheeseboard, the 76-year-old janitor, was cleaning the auditorium about 4pm. That was where the high school students sang cantatas for their families and friends each holiday. On the floor in a corner under a window, Mr. Cheeseboard saw a coiled pine-colored snake taking an afternoon nap. He rushed outdoors, got his garden hoe, and decapitated Snake before it woke up. Mr. Cheeseboard believed, "The only good snake is a dead snake." Alas another of my pets had "bit the dust."

The pet show was only a few weeks away. I lost my four baby opossums when the wind blew them away while I was transporting them by bus to the biology lab for the pet show. The day of the pet show, I found my pet minnow from the nearby stream floating on top of the water in its canning jar home. It had died the night before the pet show. I hung Minnow on a string from a stick held by a clothespin man. I won first prize. Miss Walters said my pet was the "most creative one." My younger sister, Barbetta, got second prize for a pink ribbon tied around a brown toad's neck.

Doris Weinberg

Doris with her cat, Toby

    Although Doris grew up in New Jersey and spent most of her life in Connecticut, she now enjoys her retirement years in a coastal Maine community. Once here, she joined a writer's group in Brunswick and began to emerge as a serious writer. Because of the group's positive response to her writing style, Doris was able to publish her first book.

    Her poems are very personal in nature and capture many of her life's events as well as general musings of the events around her. Although widowed and having recently lost her precious dog, Maggie, Doris has recently adopted a playful cat, Toby, and plans to include him and his amusing, yet endearing, antics in her future writings.

Doris Weinberg

A SPECIAL TREE

Trees have been around since the beginning of time
and have provided many things.
When you chop one down you can see the age,
by counting the many rings.

There is one tree that is special to me
as I was there when it got planted.
I had found a little "Polly Nose"
and brought it home, enchanted.

My dad explained it was a maple seed
that could grow and become quite tall.
And if we were very lucky,
the leaves would be red and beautiful in the fall.

He took a paper cup with soil
and planted the little seed.
We fed, watered and watched it.
Giving it everything it would need.

It soon outgrew the cup
and was transplanted to something bigger.
And I watched over it carefully
with love, prayers and vigor!

It grew nicely for a year and then Dad decided.
It was ready to be planted outside.
He picked a spot in front of our house,
and marked a circle two feet wide.

Doris Weinberg

Carefully he dug a hole and placed the tree,
which was now about twelve inches high.
Around the plant he put a tiny fence,
to protect it from passers-by.

It was slow to grow but did take root
and we measured it every year.
By the time I left home, it had nice red leaves,
and withstood weather that was severe!

The tree was about five feet tall when I left,
and my father took such pride.
And when he had to move away,
I think he felt sorry inside.

About 20 years later I was able to return.
Drove to the front of the house and parked.
The neighborhood looked very different.
But the tree was my landmark.

I sat there and stared – memories came back.
And wow! Was I amazed!
It was tall and red and beautifully shaped.
For a long time, I just stood and gazed.

My thoughts took me back to that little seed
I had once brought home with me.
And I only wished my dad was here.
He would be so proud of his lovely tree.

Doris Weinberg

PAID THE PRICE

As a young girl, my best friend was named Marie.
and we did everything together.
Our parents would see us and usually comment.
that we were birds of a feather!

She lived down the street and we'd go back and forth
playing dolls and other girl games.
There was jump rope and jacks and make believe–
popular in that time frame.

But there was one occasion that we had a fight,
and I went home angry and mad!
I went down our cellar and came back with some coal,
And proceeded to be awfully bad!

I started on the sidewalk in front of my house,
and headed in her direction.
And in each sidewalk square, using the coal,
I wrote with complete perfection.

"Marie Pauls is a Dirty Brat!!"
I wrote it in every square.
I kept it up, working very fast,
until I was almost there!

Suddenly, I saw my dad approaching,
Reading my words as he came.
And since I thought I was "Daddy's Girl,"
I suddenly felt some shame.

Doris Weinberg

He turned and walked home but soon returned,
carrying a bucket and brush.
He didn't scold but looked at me sadly
and said, "You had better rush!"

"You can't come home until all this is gone,
and remember it will soon be dark."
He turned and left me there alone,
to get rid of every mark!

I got it done and paid the price
with sore knees and a supper that turned cold.
But I did learn my lesson, that to be Daddy's girl,
I better not be twice told!

NEVER AGAIN!

My first week of college was held early
so the Freshmen could settle down.
My new roommate and I got acquainted,
and we even explored the town.

One day, during that first week,
we were invited to visit the dean.
I knew it was just a formality,
but I preferred to remain unseen.

I was extremely nervous about it,
as my roommate and I got dressed.
I really didn't want to be in his house
and act like an honored guest.

Doris Weinberg

My roommate was a smoker,
and I certainly was not.
But she suggested that when we got there,
I'd pretend I had smoked a lot.

She'd supply the cigarette
and would light it as I puffed.
I could then flick the ashes,
and try to look calm and tough.

It would keep my fingers busy
and cover up my fear.
And it would look very natural,
to anyone who was near.

We followed the plan and I drew in the puff
as she had shown me how.
But suddenly I felt very sick
with cold sweat appearing on my brow!

I raced to find the powder room
and was sick as I could be,
The dean's wife found me there,
and wiped my face so carefully.

Of course, I was humiliated
and vowed right there and then!
I would never try such a stupid thing
and I never smoked again!!

MISSING LITTLE

I was fairly young during the war–
probably between nine and thirteen.
I do remember rationing,
causing us to eat more beans!

Doris Weinberg

We made fewer trips into the city,
and my mom could not find nylons to wear.
She really disliked the rayon ones,
although she had several pairs.

Certain foods were rationed,
and we collected tin cans at school.
We even had a bomb shelter in the basement,
because that was another rule.

I remember nighttime air raid drills,
dark shades and wardens on the street.
I would watch them from my window,
thinking they were pretty neat.

I was too young to know the seriousness,
but there was one thing I really did miss.
Sugar was scarce and maybe rationed.
You would never find a Hershey's Kiss!

Chocolate syrup was made with molasses,
and it tasted pretty bad.
My favorite drink got pushed aside,
making my mother mad.

But overall, I did not miss much,
during those wartime years.
Over here we were quite blessed,
being safe and with few fears.

We've always been so fortunate,
In this great country so fine.
I certainly hope it is appreciated,
even during these turbulent times.

Doris Weinberg

"LIGHTS OUT"

It was a night my friend was with me,
and we were home alone.
I think we were about 12 years old,
when we heard an ominous tone.

It was during the war years,
and that evening, my parents went out.
We were playing a card game,
and having some fun, no doubt!

Throwing dice and eating fruit
added to our fun.
When the air raid siren did go off,
our game had just begun.

We knew just what we had to do
as we hurried up the stairs.
The lights were off, the shades were down.
On my bed I nibbled my pear.

We pulled up one shade to look outside,
And the warden was out on the street.
I think it was my neighbor patrolling.
This was his usual beat.

All was well until my friend
dropped her apple on the floor.
She turned on the light to look for it.
And the whistles became a roar!

The wardens came running and yelled at us.
I guess we committed a crime.
We turned the light off and hid under the bed.
Now I have to finish this rhyme!

My parents came home and never found out.
Of course, we did not tell.
At least the wardens didn't come up
and never rang our bell!

FINALLY, 16

There are some stages of life that are very special
and turning 16 is one.
The whole past year seemed so very slow,
that I felt as if it would never come!

But it is finally here and I'm waiting for Dad
to get home from his day at work.
I hope he's not late, today of all days!
More waiting will make me berserk!

I am finally of age and this is my dream.
It will actually raise the bar.
As soon as he's home (I will give him 10 minutes),
and then he will teach me to drive the car.

He is coming now and it won't be long,
I'll greet him with all my heart.
I'll remind him that "today's the day"
and maybe my lesson will start!

Doris Weinberg

Dad hugs my mom and then turns to me
and knows what I'm waiting for.
I am already in the driver's seat
and excitedly waiting for more.

But instead, he beckons me out of the car
and proceeds to open the hood.
"You can't drive a machine without knowing how it works."
His advice doesn't make me feel so good!

I see the battery, the crankshaft and even some plugs.
His voice goes on and on.
This isn't how I thought Lesson One would be.
Let's get in and just be gone!

I listen politely and try to remember
everything he is trying to say.
And maybe now we'll finally leave
this driveway with no more delay!

When he finally shuts the hood,
I am back in the driver's seat.
He hops right in next to me.
"Boy this is finally going to be neat"

I am all ready to go and I turn the key.
But he reaches and turns it back.
This is a stick shift car and in order to drive it,
You must first learn a difficult knack.

Off we go, bumping and jerking.
I am feeling very scared.
I thought it would be easier.
Maybe I am not really prepared!

We head to the park where there's very few cars
And I learn how to stop and start.
I am catching on and I have calmed down.
Maybe I am a little bit smart.

Doris Weinberg

It took many lessons and I passed the test.
I think driving may have been simpler then.
My Dad put in the time after work
so I could practice again and again.

Although cars today are very automatic,
Teens haven't changed a bit.
Way before they turn 16,
they are counting the days you'll admit.

My own children learned in school
and I was spared this chore.
But it still made me nervous when they took the keys
and headed out the door!

A NEW TITLE

Over 20 years ago my life
entered a brand-new stage.
My friends had already been there,
but for me, it was a new phase.

I have raised three children
and watched them grow.
If you are a parent,
this pride I am sure you know!

I saw them each grow and mature
into such fine young adults.
And maybe I did something right
to see the wonderful results!

But then I had a great experience,
I became a grandma – Lo and Behold!
I held a brand-new Becca
and my heart grew almost tenfold!

Doris Weinberg

I looked at her cute little face and
my tears caused a blur.
But when my time came to be gone,
some of me would live on in her.

And now, I can hardly believe.
She's now a wife and soon to be "Mom."
It seems to me we just shopped
for her dress for the Senior Prom!

And I'm still here, close to 90.
I'll be around for this big event.
And when I hold this new little bundle,
my heart will feel such content.

It is wonderful to know,
I haven't much longer to wait.
Because I will not only be called a grandma,
but one who is now called "Great!"

BRAVERY TAKES COURAGE

How many times do I say? "That took courage!"
A phrase that could mean different things.
An act done by someone that would scare me sufficiently,
or the terror I would know it would bring!

Doris Weinberg

Sometimes courage is shown by an act,
done without any thought.
Jumping in the river to save a child,
or gaining fame from something not sought.

I think courage is shown by foregoing something planned
in order to help someone out.
In fact, just giving of yourself for anything needed
is just what courage is about.

When did I ever show courage? Nothing comes to mind.
For me it would not be easy.
Just thinking of running into a burning building,
actually makes me queasy.

In my mind I'm a wimp with too much fear,
and I can't see myself being brave.
But I sure hope if a situation arose,
I would quickly know how to behave.

Courage really is facing your fears
and rising to any occasion.
And acting without any thought
and needing no persuasion.

For all the brave people who step up to the plate
and do it without any fuss.
They deserve our thanks and just remember,
many of them are right next to us!

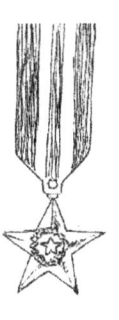

Bill Perry

Bill has loved writing for as long as he can remember. He lives in Brunswick, Maine after 35 years of living in different countries around the world. He has retired from two careers: one as a university professor and one as a manager of Peace Corps programs. Bill spent years as an academic writer and journal editor, and now enjoys writing about his life experiences. He's a native Minnesotan and, by comparison with Maine, loves the seasons in Maine without the bitter winter cold and sweltering summer heat.

Bill Perry

LIFE WITH WOOLY

I was one of the many winners in the first lottery for military service during the Vietnam War. Fortunately, I qualified for the language school in Monterey and after a year of Russian was sent to Germany to serve out the rest of my time. Shortly after arrival in Germany, my wife and I decided that we needed a dog. Our research helped us narrow the choices down to a few breeds, and availability in our area of Germany narrowed it down even more. We chose a Bedlington terrier. The moment we saw her we knew her name, probably because of her sheep-like look. We named her Wooly, brought her home and began our 16 years together.

Wooly was very smart and had no trouble adapting to our expectations for a family dog; however, our German landlords, who lived below us, didn't like Wooly even though they had agreed to our having a dog in the house. We tried to walk her in the neighborhood away from the house whenever we could, but that wasn't always possible. If we happened to take her out in the backyard, the owners would always be watching. They complained about her at every opportunity. Wooly figured out quickly that they didn't like her and growled at them whenever we met.

This unpleasant situation persisted for more than six months, so we decided to look for a new place to live. Our newspaper ad described us as "a young American couple with a small quiet dog searching for an apartment with reasonable rent." After some time, we got a phone call from a woman who said that she had a small apartment in a 200-year-old building in the center of the city. We thought that it would be worth looking at, so we met the owner in front of the apartment building the next day. The building was on a hill with tram tracks running in front and with quite a bit of traffic coming off one of the main commercial streets in town. I struggled to get through the 5-foot-five door and then negotiated the low ceilings throughout the building as we found our way up to the

Bill Perry

third floor. Bending over again, I stepped into the small furnished apartment heated by coal and with an unheated toilet in a small room on the outdoor balcony. There was a kitchen next to the balcony in the back; the bedroom and the living room were on the warmer, noisy side of the apartment.

Wooly really liked the owner, and the owner liked Wooly. In an unforgettable moment, we told her that the apartment was perfect for us. She looked at us and said, "I will rent it to you because I like your dog so much." This was the beginning of our new life in the city with Wooly. I got used to the small doors and low ceilings; we got used to the coal heat, the tram and the traffic noise, as well as the freezing cold winter trips out to the toilet on the balcony. Wooly was happy and that made us happy.

Most of our transportation was by bicycle. I wasn't sure how Wooly would adapt to traveling by bike, but I thought I it was worth a try. I found an old plastic beer crate, cut out the dividers and put in a cardboard floor to which we could add cushions to make the ride more comfortable for her. I used a variety of nuts, bolts and clamps to fasten the box to the back of my bike and was finally ready to take Wooly on a test ride through the city. She loved the box and after that always looked forward to trips on the back. Only once in all of her years with us did she jump out of the box. That was during a rainstorm and about six inches of water had accumulated in the box. Guess I would have jumped out, too.

Bill Perry

One memorable adventure with Wooly was our ski trip to Garmisch in southern Germany. By this time, Wooly went with us everywhere—to restaurants, to visit friends, on trips around Germany, so why would we not take her along us on our ski trip to the Alps. Of course, there was never a problem having a dog in restaurants, hotels or other public places, so traveling with her on the train to Garmisch and staying in the hotel was completely acceptable. But what about on the ski slopes? We decided to give it a try.

We bought our weekly pass for skiing that included some cable car lifts and a few T-bars. When we asked if the dog could go with us, the people in the ticket booth said that it wasn't common, but certainly wasn't a problem. Wooly was dressed in her winter sweater and ready to go skiing for the first time. I can still remember the excitement in her body as I skied down the mountainside holding her under my arm. After a few runs, we decided to take turns skiing and staying with her at the chalet. Each day was about the same—she liked the experience but also really enjoyed the attention she got in the chalet.

Near the end of my service, my parents came to Europe to visit us and to revisit the route that my father had walked during World War II from Naples, Italy to the Brenner Pass in Austria. After spending some time together at our apartment in Germany and a side-trip to the Disney castle in southern Germany, we began to re-trace his wartime steps. About a week into the trip, it became clear that my father and Wooly didn't get along very well. If we asked him to take her on a walk, she would simply stop in the most inappropriate places, like the middle of the street, and seemed to be doing everything that she could to embarrass him. She was very good at it! When he began calling her "that damned dog," it was apparent that we would have to watch both of them closely.

117

Bill Perry

My father seemed to be jealous of the attention that Wooly got everywhere we went. Our stop in Venice was a good example of this. When we arrived at our hotel, the clerk said that they had a perfect room for us—the one that Elizabeth Taylor and Richard Burton had slept in. My father's face lit up with joy and expectation, and then they gave the key to my wife and me saying that they thought our dog would really enjoy the room.

This tension continued throughout the trip and culminated in Amsterdam, the last stop of their visit. My father was excited to have a chance to visit the Heineken brewery, although he was never a beer drinker. On the day we had set aside for the tour, the brewery happened to be closed, so we had to change our plans. Dad was very disappointed, but the other three of us were happy to have had a chance to go to the Rijksmuseum instead. My father hated museums, so we knew that he would opt to stay in the car, and of course, no dogs were allowed in the museum. Three hours later we returned to the car only to see my father smoking like a chimney in the driver's seat and Wooly sitting as far away from him as she could in the back seat. From that moment on, they never even looked at each other. I still wonder what happened while we were on our museum visit that day.

After several years in Minnesota and Wisconsin, Wooly lived out the rest of her life in her native Germany. We had had our first child in Germany, and Wooly was always there to play with him and protect him. When our second child was born 10 years later, Wooly seemed happy about it at first, but then must have felt a shift in attention to the children away from her. Ours relationship became more distant. This may have happened because being home with the children, I focused a lot of my attention on them. Wooly always went out on walks with us and on family trips, but something was different. I felt bad about the growing distance, but didn't know how to deal with it, so I didn't.

By age 16, Wooly had lost a lot of her energy. Sometimes she would pee in the house, so we set up an area of the apartment specifically for her and also put extra sheets on the bed where she slept. Yes, she no longer slept with us, especially with the new baby, who was constantly in our bed. One morning I went to the area where Wooly slept and called to her to go for our walk. She was often slow in getting out of the bed at her age, but this time she didn't move. I kept calling and then touched her—she was cold and stiff. Dead.

Our wonderful years with Wooly had come to an end. She knew us as a couple, then with one child and then two. She had gone everywhere with us during her 16 years and had brought so much enjoyment into our lives. Now she was gone and a bit of us was gone with her. My wife and I decided that we wouldn't get another dog. It would be too painful. But within a month, we were in the Black Forest at a breeder's home looking for our next Wooly.

SLEEPLESS IN JAPAN

We had been living in Miyazaki, Japan for over a year, enjoying our life on the floor—no furniture except a kitchen table and chairs, and the routines of a warm kotatsu (a family table on the floor with a heater under it) in the evening, a hot bath before bed, and the warmth of a futon on tatami. Such fond memories.

Then one night at about 4 AM, I heard a dog in the neighborhood barking. Thought the barking would stop, but it didn't. It continued until around 7. Hoping that the incessant barking wouldn't continue the next night, I went to bed less relaxed than usual. Promptly at 4 AM, it started again. This pattern continued for a week before I decided that I needed to do something about it. I was playing tennis regularly, so there were lots of tennis balls around the house. As a former baseball player, I had a relatively good arm, so was prepared for the night-time barking marathon. I found a good angle for targeting the dog from our bathroom window and once the barking started, I began throwing tennis balls. He was surprised at first and then decided that it was a game. He began retrieving the balls and piling them in the corner of his owner's driveway. Then when I stopped throwing the balls, he started barking again. Back to my bed with eyes wide open.

I began doing research on barking dogs and learned that dog whistles were often quite effective. Shortly after reading the research, I headed for the local hardware store and purchased a dog whistle. Full of hope for quiet, I woke up at 4 AM to the bark of

Bill Perry

the dog. I ran to the window and began blowing the whistle. There was a short silence and then the barking resumed at a higher volume. The dog seemed to enjoy the sound. I tried this routine for a few more days. My "indoor" dog hated the sound and would run to a corner of the house to hide whenever I blew the whistle. Another apparent failure.

My next step was to order a sound-activated device that was guaranteed to keep dogs from barking. I mounted it on the outside of the house and was so excited for that night's session with the dog. 4 AM came, the dog started barking and then stopped abruptly. I went back to bed and slept well for the first time in a long time. Problem solved. I was proud of myself for finding a solution. After three days of quiet, the dog was back at his 4 AM hour. I thought maybe the batteries in the device were dead, but no, everything was working. I began to think that I was challenging a super-dog. Nothing worked.

I asked my wife, who knew the local culture well, what we could do. She suggested that we contact City Hall. Their environmental department dealt with neighborhood issues like this. Of course, being in Japan, we couldn't just go to the neighbors and ask them to keep their dog quiet, although that would have been the most natural thing for me to do at this point. A representative from City Hall came to our house and was very sympathetic about the issue. She said that she would include a note about the problem in the neighborhood newsletter. I was so happy that some action was being taken. When the newsletter came out, it said something like "if you have a dog and if that particular dog barks at inconvenient hours, please stop it from barking." End of story.

Several other neighbors were aware of the barking problem and praised my efforts. I felt like a local hero. The dog continued to bark, though. Nothing changed for weeks and one evening as I was complaining to my family, my four-year-old daughter, as a born Buddhist, said very simply, "Daddy, just don't hear the dog." I smiled and realized something new about my Western attention to the world around me. I have continued working on her suggestion, but it has been a difficult journey across cultures to be able to tune out the noise.

The dog died mysteriously a week later.

Bill Perry

LOVE AT FIRST SIGHT

My final service posting with the Peace Corps was in Kosovo, a newly independent, primarily Muslim country in the Balkans. The country had been recently bombed by NATO to force the Serbs to retreat from the Kosovar-Albanian territory, and in spite of the post-conflict damage, the local people were overjoyed to have the war come to an end. The Albanian-Kosovars were so happy about having been liberated from the Serbs that even my name, Bill, conjured up positive images as they thought about their liberator, Bill Clinton. Having lived among the Serbs in Belgrade in the former Yugoslavia for a number of years before that time, I was always intrigued by Kosovo, and pleased that good fortune had brought me to the capital city, Pristina, where I helped start the first Peace Corps Volunteer program.

As a US government employee with some diplomatic perks, I settled into a beautiful three-floor house with a balcony overlooking the city. The balcony faced east, so I routinely enjoyed coffee on sunny mornings on the balcony before walking to my hectic workplace in the city. At work I grappled with the daily problems of Volunteers and new staff working in a cross-cultural setting where there had never been any kind of volunteer program and where family ties were so tight that having a foreigner live in a homestay for two years was beyond belief.

After several months in my new home, a sanctuary from work, I first became aware of a type of blackbird unique to Central Europe, the kos. I learned that the name of the country, Kosovo, meant "field of blackbirds," but was unaware of how my future relationship with the kos would develop.

This relationship began one sunny morning when I went outside with my cup of coffee and saw that the entire balcony was covered with bird droppings. There wasn't a bird in sight, so I decided to investigate the change. Within a few days, I discovered that a large group of kos was visiting my balcony in the mornings, seemingly chatting with each other for about 30 minutes, leaving droppings everywhere and then departing. But where were they going after the visit?

Further investigation revealed that they had a daily routine, at least in the warmer months, during which they would spend time

Bill Perry

with their families at a park on the top of the hill above my house. I visited that park and discovered over 100 nests, all constructed in the same way. It was mating season, so I saw the frenzied activity of the birds, especially the males. They were so noisy that it was impossible hear other humans speaking. The males flew around the nests seemingly to protect the females and the eggs. It was an unforgettable multisensory experience for me.

But the mystery remained—why were they visiting my balcony in the early morning? After more local investigation, I learned that the males would fly to the city in the late afternoons and sleep in the large, cool trees along the main boulevard. Their white droppings could be seen under the trees where they had slept. Then in the mornings they would go back to the top of the hill to spend time with their families. Made sense to me.

However, I wasn't at all happy with their having chosen my balcony as a stopover on the way home from the city—it was a tedious clean-up job each day. I decided to do some research on their habits and maybe discover a way to keep them away from my balcony.

A common approach to deter blackbirds such as the kos was to mount shiny mylar strips in the area where they roosted. I went to the local hardware store, bought a sheet of mylar, cut it into strips and then hung the strips above the railing of the balcony. Having hoped that the mylar would keep the kos away, I was sorely disappointed that it had had a completely different effect on them—they loved the shiny mylar. There was an even larger group of kos chatting on my balcony the next morning.

I went back to the research and decided to use my diplomatic privilege of ordering from Amazon through the American Embassy to order a plastic owl. The owl was about a foot tall and was to be filled with either sand or water for stability. Perhaps this would solve my problem.

10 days later, the package from Amazon arrived at the Embassy, bringing me high expectations and a touch of joy. I set up the owl that day, and the next morning, the kos had disappeared. Up to that point, I had only heard about how owls were feared by other birds, and

now there was proof. The kos were gone, probably frightened by the plastic owl, and I could resume my morning coffee and sunrise routine.

About a week later, I went out with my coffee and looked up to my right to see a small owl in the rafters—a real owl! I hurried back into the house, scared and wondering why this little owl was perched above my balcony. Then I realized that the small owl was probably in love, in love with my plastic owl. The next morning, I peeked up into the rafters and yes, the little owl was still there. After a few days of observation, it became clear that the real owl would spend the day with my plastic owl under its gaze, and then fly off at night to do whatever owls do in the dark.

I finally summoned my courage and decided to have coffee with both of the owls, the plastic and the real. Mornings became enjoyable again with the three of us sitting on the balcony watching the sun come up over the mountains. But this morning delight was short-lived. About two weeks after the three of us had bonded, I went out for the morning ritual, and the plastic owl was down—its head pecked beyond recognition. And the little owl was gone, gone never to return.

I have spent years trying to figure out what happened and still am not sure, but my guess is that the real owl finally decided that it was time to take a risk and declare its love for the plastic owl. There must have been great disappointment when the two came together for that brief moment before the plastic owl was pecked to pieces. Love at first sight is a lot more complex than most of us think—just ask the little owl.

Bill Perry

HERE COME THE CROWS

My move to Bucharest after retiring from the Peace Corps brought many surprises—one of the most memorable was my life on the balcony. The apartment was on the fifth floor with large rooms, high ceilings and spectacular views of a lush park in the center of Bucharest.

One late afternoon on a very sunny fall day, I went out onto the balcony to do my crosswords and to take in the fresh air of the park. I could see children on their way home from school and working people hurrying home, but the majority of the park visitors were simply enjoying the beauty of nature in the center of this bustling metropolis.

As my gaze drifted skyward, I saw several crows flying seemingly searching for a place to roost in the trees facing the apartment. Then came more crows, then more and before long, there were hundreds of crows flying overhead and cawing to the top of their lungs. I stopped reading and simply stared at this wild scene, wondering if it was a regular occurrence in the park. After asking some local residents about the crows, I learned that during the warmer part of the year, they came every evening to sleep in the trees—all of this after a hard day at the city dump miles away. At that point, I decided to study the behavior of the crows through reading, observation, and conversations with the neighbors. Each day I would sit on the balcony and look forward to the crows' return to the park, and most days I learned something new about their behavior. It was apparent that their routines were not random. I also paid attention to their intra-group interactions.

My balcony time soon became a routine—I would do crossword puzzles, waiting for the arrival of the crows. If they were a few minutes late, I would become concerned. It was a treasured time that evolved into my daily meditation. One to two hours became the norm for my balcony time. I found peace with the hundreds of crows flying and cawing as they sought their nighttime shelter.

Bill Perry

One evening I noticed that one of the two-hundred some crows was injured, and then observed how the crows not only kept other kinds of birds away from the injured one, but also seemed to be providing aid to the fallen member of their "murder." A murder of crows? Why not a flock? There are many stories and superstitions about crows related to dark things like death, hangings, and the like, but a murder?

Then I saw it. Or at least I thought I saw and heard it. The injured crow was crying in pain and then after it had been surrounded by other crows, the painful crying changed to a final cry of life. The injured crow was dead. Did they kill it or did it simply die?

A few months later, I had a one-on-one encounter with a crow from that murder on my way to the swimming pool. It was spring, and I was casually walking through a different park on the way to swim. I spied a pair of crows mating in a tree next to the path and looked closely at them.

Then as I continued walking—whap, I felt a hard thump on my black backpack. One of the crows had attacked me. I looked up in time to see that the bird was making a second dive, this time hitting my backpack in the center. I picked up my pace and headed for the nearest tree to take cover, fear coursing through my body as the crow dived at me for the third time.

I waited under the branch until the coast was clear, and then quickly made my way to the main street. The whole time I was thinking about what could have triggered this response from the crow. My first thought was that I had embarrassed the couple by glancing at the mating ritual, but that seemed to be too much of a human reason. I determined to do more research after swimming. I kept thinking about crows and murder, but wasn't sure how it could be a part of the answer to why I was attacked.

My reading on the reasons crows might attack humans revealed numerous possibilities, but one stood out to me—the one related to dead crows. The research suggested that if crows see an outsider removing the carcass of a dead crow, they will attack. Then I thought about my black backpack, and I knew the answer. It wasn't an embarrassed crow or simply a crazy bird, it was a noble crow defending the honor of a departed species-mate. Mystery solved and my love of crows restored. These days whenever I hear criticism of crows, I go right to this story to help the critic understand what marvelous creatures they are. There is so much to learn from these special birds.

Quoth the Crow "Nevermore."

A CHANGE OF HEART

From my earliest memory, I did not like my father. He had been in Italy fighting the Germans when my older sister was born, and when he returned, he did his best to become a part of her life and also to get to know my mother as his lifelong partner. I was born three years after he returned, in what was probably a very difficult time for him. My mother had lost two brothers during the war, and they had married right before he left for the front and had a daughter while he was gone. A daunting life lie ahead of him when he returned. He had completed only three years of college when he left and needed to find a job, especially with a new baby, me.

Dad didn't have much time for me given the pressures he felt from trying to find the right job to provide for his family. It's hard to imagine the pain he must have lived with after his wartime car accident. He was hospitalized for two months in Italy, but never revealed any of the details to me. There was no question, though, that he was dedicated to his family, to making sure that we had a good place to live and that we could enjoy the basics of middle-class life. I needed more attention than he could give me, though, so I turned to my grandfather, who was more than happy to have a

Bill Perry

grandson eager to learn the values of the white world of Minnesota.

Watching American football, smoking, and drinking were my father's primary joys in life. I tried hard to find ways to please him: playing football in high school and college, working at the company he had become devoted to and always looking for ways that his life could become a healthier one. I remember coming back from my first long-term stay in Germany in the Army hoping that he would want to ride bikes with me. His response to my overtures was to laugh. He said that it would never happen.

We had a frightening showdown about my career when after a few years working at his company, I told him that I wanted to become a teacher. He was angry and revealed his stereotype of teachers as men whose shirt collars were tattered and whose ties never matched their jackets. His reaction scared me and finally put the distance between us that had been looming for years. This distance remained until his death.

So why the change of heart now, forty years later? On a trip to Minnesota, I was sorting through photos, albums and letters from the past century with my sister in preparation for her move to North Carolina when she handed me a package of letters that my father had written to my mother during the War—my heart melted. For the first time, I saw my father as a person who was in love and who had dreams for the future for himself and his family. His letters revealed the hardships of day-to-day battles with the Germans, his experiences of loss when friends fell in the War, and his hopes for a bright future with my mother. Each letter, accompanied by photos, helped me to see the struggles of a strong, attractive man who had grown up in a military boarding school without parents. He had finally found the love of his life. The letters brought his dreams to life—something I had never been aware of during my years with him.

I left Minnesota for Maine with this package of letters and with scans of his childhood photo album. I also found photos from his business career. I have new enthusiasm to learn who my father really was and, perhaps in the process, to learn more about who I really am. Forgiveness of the past is never easy, but for me it is an opportunity to see more deeply into my own heart.

Carol Smith Markell

Carol and her dog, Calliegh

    Carol is a native Mainer – born, raised and educated in Van Buren. She graduated from Mercy Hospital School of Nursing, an RN after three years of training and two six-month affiliations at hospitals in D.C. and Baltimore. With State of Maine public health nursing guidance, she set up a new community and school health system in a mill town of over six thousand residents. She then married and became the mom of two healthy children. Years later, when her children were in college, she went through a four-year college program earning a BA in English and Behavioral Science.

    Carol has been writing almost from the time she learned to read. Adventures were her best friends growing up – whether engaged in an actual one, reading about it or imagining it! Those four college years of studying, writing, and being critiqued and mentored were fulfilling and fun.

    It was there that she felt drawn to write about whatever subject she chose to write doing so as the oldest student in those classes! She discovered the joy of setting herself free to burrow into facts, fiction, and her imagination, to let her mind wander through it all, and at the end to find that she actually liked what she wrote. Her writing is what leads her every day to be curious, to want to know more about everything. She is grateful to have the opportunity to share her writing to the supportive group in the **Write On Writers** class at People Plus.

Carol Smith Markell

TREASURES

Books and jewelry, **china** and crystal
All things I value and widely esteem.
But, none so much as two in number,
My son and daughter!

How so they exist?
By love of God
And force of will.

A click of the camera, an instant tale told
Of glowing smiles, tears shed, losses counted,
Blunders survived and fences mended,
Mountains skied and obstacles surmounted.

Photographs fill the oddly sized albums
Rendering moments from sunshine to sadness
To sparkling stars against dark skies –
Memories captured, now seemingly ageless.

Hark to all parents!
Present and future
Near and far.

Children are our unheralded national treasures.
The rearing of their life, the relinquishing of our life,
The production, investment and involvement with,
The discovery of a prize, that each child is a precious gem.

Take care of them
Love from all depths
Make golden each day
And remember…

**they will soar away, and on their own path,
treasuring all you bestowed.**

Carol Smith Markell

LIGHT SO BRIGHT

On a late Sunday morning, my sister and I jumped into the canoe on River Tole with our lunch basket in hand. We were headed downstream, about two miles away, to a picnic site overlooking Great Falls. The river path to the falls was a gentle, curving and ambling ride with low banks of brush, wildflowers and meadow land within close sight. If others had heard us, they would have thought the laughter and chuckles were coming from children. We were bubbling over with a sense of hilarity and happiness, the lighthearted feeling children experience.

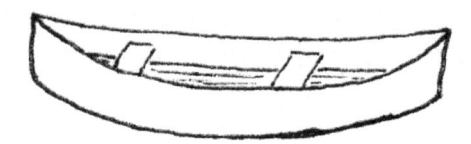

As we dipped our oars into the water infrequently and enough to hold the canoe on course, we chatted happily about yesterday's family gathering held at our uncle's cottage. My sister and I had escaped the rest of the family for an afternoon of catching up. With only fifteen months between us, we had been so close until marriage to a wonderful man transported her from Maine to Seattle. Now reunited after seven years apart, it was a time for renewing bonds and reviving the old memories of treasured and not so treasured moments.

The birds competed with us for attention during this rare moment of togetherness. We both had four children, and the more we talked about all of them, the louder the birds seemed to chirp, letting us know we were invading their quiet neighborhood and that we were not welcome to stay. We slid downstream for almost an hour over calm waters, the ride smooth and gentle. The sun shone bright from a clear blue sky. Everything was peaceful, warm, and almost hypnotizing in its perfection. Our attention remained focused on each other, catching up on old news, bits of gossip, and the private, personal details of lives that cannot be shared on the phone.

Carol Smith Markell

All of a sudden, we both heard the rushing noise of the falls, and stared at each other in shock. As part of our past lifeguard training, we immediately went into action. Despite our efforts to fight the current, the downstream pull persisted. Even together, in perfect form doing backstrokes with our oars, the pull was too strong for us. I turned to face the front of the canoe as it tipped forward and was propelled downward over the top of the falls. There was no time to scream, no time to plead or pray. In one fell swoop, the canoe's trajectory was decided and the hapless were helpless to change its course. The sound was a warning that had come too late for preventive action.

As I fell into churning and angry water, it seemed to rise up to meet me too quickly and with resolute ferocity. Down I spiraled into the water, continuing down and further down into its deep darkness, the water surrounding me and protecting me from physical pain. The shock of the unexpected turn of events somewhat cushions the mind, but it does not obliterate the memory of being airborne and down-spouted, nor does it erase the image of my hands searching desperately for something to cling to, a tree, a limb, a rock. Not finding it, panic overwhelmed me with a band-like constriction of the throat. While I gurgled my way to the bottom, any sound that I might have intended to make was silenced. I felt the motion much like a leaf in the wind would, helpless to change its course, inert, and victim to a more powerful source than I was.

Carol Smith Markell

Time passed, and when I was able to open my eyes, it was to a bright light inviting me to stroll through its tunnel. I was at peace and I knew everything now. But strangely, I felt a presence near me, behind me, and with temerity I turned my head to the side. Instead of the stranger I expected, I saw my sister. There we stood, looking at each other momentarily, and finally I offered her my hand. We stood shoulder to shoulder for a time. Then hand in hand, we commenced our walk toward the beckoning light and the path that lay ahead.

CALLEIGH

Can you stop a fistful of water from dripping from your hand?
Can your hand hold for long the sifting white beach sand?
I need to use a sieve to catch all the words that bend
Sufficiently into a true representation of my dear dog.

A red cocker spaniel weighing twenty pounds
Is a sweet earthen angel even at age ten
She traveled from Louisiana for better,
Coming to Maine at age 1½, I rescued her.

Bubbling with puppy love, so well trained,
A gift at first sight, her goodness ingrained
From the skill of her master, a soldier whose plight
Was serving his third Army deploy now inflight.

She has become even dearer to me and to you,
Everyone she meets stops and compliments accrue
While she wags her tail and stretches up for a kiss.
Her gifts abound, we accept with unfounded bliss.

When freed, she runs like the wind, floppy ears at play,
Her maneuvers like a plane rising from the runway.
Yet, a call from her mistress and she stops on the trail
And returns home happily wagging her tail.

Carol Smith Markell

Still a purveyor of love, she is always able to connect
And I have not yet ruined her, though I'm far from perfect.
My eyes see understanding in those brown eyes of hers
Whether they ask for food or shed tears for mine or yours.

This dear little loving **spaniel**
is my ticket to heaven.
This I say because she is a gift,
sheer goodness in motion.

A SUNSET'S BRILLIANCE

One evening I drove to Ferry Beach, about five miles from my condo. The drive over the curvy Black Point Road in Scarborough was visually stimulating. I rode by individual beach homes and a beach home community interspersed with patchworks of open fields, planted fields and copses of pine. Turning into the street leading up to the beach, I felt a tension ebbing from me, like a current draining it all away. Ferry Beach offered easy parking, an L-shaped white sand beach now at low tide, and a much-used dock. It was an early evening, with the sun slowly setting – the end of a perfectly cloudless day with temps in the upper 70s. It was a favorite place of mine to watch the day come to a end, to find that calm, that peace that can be as flighty as a feather in the wind.

At the right end of the beach is a dock used by commercial fishermen with a boat launch for private sailing adventures. That is where I sat, **halfway** up the dock, dangling my legs like a happy child, observing tidal action and minute fish battling the pull of the tide. As I looked westward at the huge ball of a darkening yellow, I knew I had arrived just in time.

I was lost in an abundance of miscellaneous thoughts when I heard running foot strikes on the thick wooden planks coming from my left, with each step being a pronounced sound. Then, to my right, I felt a presence, and I heard a voice say, "Hi." I looked up and saw a young male, small in stature, smiling down at me. He said, "I'm Anthony," and without an invitation sat down next to me – comfortable and unconcerned that I had not yet invited him.

Carol Smith Markell

He asked what my name was. I said, "Carol." He was sitting so close to me that I wondered if his vision was impaired. I heard calling from the beach and saw a woman near the dock's land edge, signaling as to whether he was bothering me. I shook my head and smiled.

His youthful face was speckled with freckles the size and color of new pennies, like my dad's face was when he was a child. Anthony's head was topped with brown hair in a crew cut. But more noticeable than the freckles and his hair were his exuberant grin and his blue-green eyes that slanted upward. His sturdy little voice matched his body, firm and solid. Though he was about eight years old, he was smaller in stature than the normal 8-year-old, appearing not like a willful child but rather purposeful one. He seemed so comfortable near me, confident that he was in the right place with a friend.

He began talking to me as if he was bringing me up to date about what had been happening in his life. In the next several minutes, I learned that he had received a tetanus shot a few weeks before, and other shots in his arm a few weeks before that. He pointed out scratches on his leg that he said didn't hurt as much as the shots did. Using his short stubby fingers for additional expression, he told me about his mother and family. He shared that he had a 14-year-old sister, a 9-year-old sister and that his mother was over 40. To the left of me, he pointed them out on the beach, his fingers crossing close to my nose. He seemed so proud of them.

He asked to see my face. I faced him and he quietly observed. I was wearing sunglasses and a sun hat that covered my hair and hid some of my face. He gestured for me to remove my sunglasses, and then my hat too. I didn't. It was almost as if he was trying to memorize my face and it felt invasive.

"I want to see your face," he said again, raising his hand, a gentle move, toward my cheek. I turned to look at him. He turned to me, the sunglasses forgotten, and began a serious inquiry, with one question following the other in rapid fire.

"Where do you live?" I told him I lived about three miles away. "Do you have a dog?" and "What kind of dog is it?" and "What's its name?" and "Where is it?" and "Do you have children?" and "How many?" and "What are their names?" and "Where do they live?" Then he asked if I had a husband. Without awaiting the answer, he then asked, "Where is he?" and "Does he have a beard?"

Then he grimaced, looking up at me and scrunching the features of his face in a tight knot. At this point, the next question became too intrusive. He asked, "Why is your husband at home instead of being here with you?" I didn't answer. He asked the question again. Instead of answering, I drew his attention to the descending sun. The questions about my husband, so innocently asked, bored uncomfortably into the loneliness I was feeling. But he didn't give up. When he asked me again why I was there alone, I looked out at the incoming tidal activity. I was tempted to lie. The questions were direct, but I knew they were not intended to be invasive. He had no idea he was traversing in private space.

How does one handle a situation when a child is unaware and incapable of understanding that he is pushing boundaries? My reaction to his last question was to divert his attention again by asking what his mother and sisters were doing. I looked at him and saw a hurt, puzzled look in his eyes. He just could not understand why I wasn't answering the question, why my husband wouldn't want to be here with me when he was so happy to be with me. With tears and a feeling of humility, I finally answered, "My husband and I are no longer married."

In the next moment, we were joined by one of his sisters and then the other, and they both tried to convince him to go to the end of the dock to rejoin them. He stubbornly stayed by my side. Finally, his mother came. Even in the presence of his mom, a healthy, lean woman with kind and intelligent eyes, he still wanted to be with me. I asked her why Anthony wanted me to remove my sunglasses. His mother said, "He just wants to look into your eyes." Now I understood why he sensed I was not compliant about his question of my husband. I understood why he felt lost. Though the sunglasses shielded my eyes from the sun, they also prevented him from seeing my expressions. The clues, eye expressions he was accustomed to, were missing. He thought that by removing the sunglasses he would find the pathway back to me. To the deaf, lip-reading is a communication tool. To Anthony, looking into someone's eyes is a communication tool as effective as when sunlight filters through obstructing branches, giving clarity to its observers.

His mother told him, "Come now. Your sisters and I are going out to get an ice cream." A wide grin infused his face with the light of excitement. But before he turned away, I took off my sunglasses and sun hat. He bent down to give me a huge hug and looked me right in the eyes as he said goodbye, waving back joyfully to me as he followed his mom.

I remained, my feet still dangling from the dock, my heart clothed in a rare peace, my thoughts enlivened about what can happen in fifteen short minutes. This stranger, a young lad of eight, gave me the gift of his heart on a platter, without expectation of return or worry of harm. I will die humbled by the experience, but richer for the change it evoked within and the lasting memory it created. May God bless him, wherever he is.

A FISH, GUN AND DRIVE TALE

My father took me fishing once in his life. It was far from what I would describe as a rousing success for several reasons. It was a blistering hot June day with the unrelenting sun beating down on us. The lake was choppy from a wind gusting its force with what felt like a searing heat on thin, delicate skin. The fish we sought were asleep somewhere and not biting on his hook or mine. The final disruption to a peaceful afternoon were the three hours of being afloat in a narrow canoe – a bit too much solitude for a teenager. My Dad deserves an A plus for his attempt, but this was the last time I was invited to join him. And I know I would have declined a follow-up invitation from him had he asked me.

My poor Dad! He also tried to teach me how to shoot, another one of his hobbies. On a beautiful cloudless day, we went up to the target practice range on his farmland. His patient instructions on how to hold a rifle were clear, but my reaction to the noise coming from the actual gunshot, even though I expected it, was to jump. Well, we all know what happened next…the rifle butt hit my shoulder hard enough to knock me down and I let out a yell. Tears followed and that experience also was never repeated.

There is one success story from my father's efforts to be a good dad and that is the driving lesson when I was fourteen. He took me up to the potato field dirt roads, and settled me on a high cushion in the driver's seat. I drove the car around the sometimes hilly, sometimes flat terrain, that was interspersed with narrow and winding dirt roads. I still remember the enjoyment I felt at being in command at the helm. Imagine the power surge this tall teen felt while driving, maneuvering the brakes and accelerator on a standard shift for the first time. Dad sat in the center of the seat, ready to offset any problem that might arise. But this was one experience that was successful from beginning to end. When I came to a skinny stream, I accelerated and traversed it quickly. He was actually so proud on me for gunning the accelerator rather than braking, slowing down or stopping in the stream. What a good dad he was!

MY GRADY

As time grows short, I pen his tale that's mine
About my boy, an aging Cocker Spaniel lad.
He's black with eyes of brown, a perfect snout
That'll win your heart and mine every time.
We think of him as just a 'lil old puppy
But truth be told, he's over the age of ninety.
He sports the white beard of age and a jaw with spaces
And seems to smile his way thru bushes and brambles.
He flies down the stairs, his little pink tongue showing
As he sniffs the grass and every whiff in the air,
So, we watch as he prances and dances to song
As if to show us all that age doesn't matter a darn.
He's deaf, nearly blind but wears a twinkle in his eye.
He's my Grady boy, who brings nothing but joy and more!

Carol Smith Markell

THE LOST CAMERA

She walked forward, each foot a leaden weight. Had she walked down the forested path before forgetting her camera yesterday, her movements would have seemed as effortless as the flight of condors. Had she been on this journey during daytime hours, each of her steps would have danced over the rays of light. But now it was still dark.

The darkness rang loud in her body, deafening any musical cadence that might have softened her fearful thoughts. Groping her way uncertainly with stultifying feelings in her chest, her fear had gelled into rock form and she felt as if there were walls closing in on her. Much like the recruit whose drill sergeant repeatedly barks out the command "your right foot in front of your left," she lifted each foot and moved forward as if ahead she would be facing an enemy. She *knew* why she was **going**. She *knew* where she had to go. She *knew* that what she had left behind was safe and that she would return home. But, she was worried that time might fail her.

She walked on, the miles accruing, and when the first rays of light shimmered over the hillside, she saw what she had come for, a panorama of high hills, a valley and a stream below, awash in misty muted tones that were veiled in mysterious nuances. She was now in a heightened state of readiness, her camera focused on the tremulous daylight shedding its first beams. In the next few moments, she had captured the beauty she discerned visually with simple snaps of the aperture, beauty that she had tried to share with him orally.

Eyes brimming with tears of excitement, she ran back down the path, her steps light as she traveled the five miles back to their home. In the cool early morning temperatures, her running breath was like the hoar frost that coated each dark pink rose in the garden. She breezed through the door and into the studio to develop her sunrise images, fiddling impatiently with the film in the developing solution. As she awaited the process, she thought about how she lost her camera in the marketplace yesterday. Had she not found it two hours later at the police station when she drove the twenty miles back to the marketplace, this past night's journey to the wild sanctuary would not have happened.

The photos were everything she had hoped for and she hurried upstairs to show him. It was his dying wish that he see the sunrise on top of the hillside that overlooked the Twin Rivers fork he had so often visited and, as he slipped in and out of consciousness, she prayed that her gift to him was the best work she had ever done. As his eyes fluttered open, she lifted the display of eight large photos on a photo board. He reached for her nearby hand, and a gentle knowing smile crossed his face as his eyes beheld the beauty for as long as he could. Little by little, time edged away the moments, and he slipped away slowly with the residual of a smile remaining on his face after he had passed.

THE YEAR IS 2563...

Five hundred and forty-two years later, I am hovering overhead, looking down at the radical transformation of one of the areas I knew so well – the state of Maine. Much of it is now underwater, its mountain peaks no longer common and its forests no longer a sight. Ice has covered most of its breadth and width, with the shoreline Maine was known for now unremarkable. Looking down, I realized that time has its own natural power and nothing remains the same. Time does away with structures, shapes, solitude and security. As human beings, we live in what can be termed a moment of time, riding on the waves of life while awaiting the final wave that takes us up on a celestial journey or down to the underworld teeming with heat.

Although I passed away and flew up to sunnier meadows many, many years ago, I have been working the skies as an investigator. When I had first arrived at the pearly gates, I white-knuckled myself into an interview with St. Petra for a job. I did not want to be lodged for a lifetime on a golden throne. I waited at the main gate for what seemed like a long time until the Woman herself showed up.

St. Petra walked me to her studio for a meeting with the HR interviewer. The interviewer sat there looking like a youngster compared to everyone else I saw up here. I'd say she was about twenty-seven years old and surprisingly she felt the need to draw thick lines of red on her lips, way too much lipstick for my taste. She introduced herself as Gretchen and told me of the two job offerings she had: one was at a food distribution center for the handicapped; the other was for an investigator to find the lost souls who escaped the space station near Planet Omicron.

Because research has always yanked at my interests, I opted for the detective job. Then I continued on, oddly feeling like I had to sell my skills, and told her of my innate curiosity, my love of research and my thrill at learning new things. She listened, with the patience of Job and without fidgeting throughout my three-minute dialogue. My mind, overwhelmed with the moment, veered to wondering if we achieve instant perfection like hers when we walk through the pearly gates. Gretchen certainly appeared to be angelic, though without the wings I expected angels to have.

Her calm voice broke into my reverie. She asked, "Can you ride a horse?"

I was unprepared for what I thought this question was about – my social activities. My mind locked itself into a stunned silence and I had no answer. She continued, asserting that horseback riding was part of the job. With a smile, she told me that riding sky horses like Pegasus was fun. They were winged and a dazzling color of white. They were gentle and always eager to help. Because they were divine animals of ultimate perfection, they would never throw a rider. At that point, I felt it was safe to tell her I had never ridden a horse, but would enjoy doing so. Pegasus' life was short-lived but the Greek god Zeus honored all the sky horses with special gifts. After their job is done, their life ends and they sail into the night skies to be an incandescent luminary, a tiny body of light forever glowing like the sun.

Since my hiring, I have sought and found lost souls, a few I even knew. I don't know how old I am at this point nor do I care, because I am loving my job and the atmosphere up here, and I am grateful to be reunited and reuniting with all the people whom I have loved. Not a bad place to be with its balmy temperature, a tad better than the other final destination, a place known for its miserable heat.

Robert Mulligan

Robert, a resident of Bath, Maine, loves living in the Midcoast area. Born in New York City he subsequently has lived in almost all of the northeast states, as well as a few other regions. His 30 years in the airline industry took him to many parts of the world but he was always happy to return home.

The next decade in software design was more US-based, which allowed more time with family. After retirement he continued to serve in various positions at a yoga and health center, an art museum and as a substitute teacher, while volunteering in Senior Advocacy roles with AARP.

At home with wife Audrey, and cats Lulu and Casey, Bob enjoys writing, cooking, hiking, skiing, gardening, the surrounding rivers, lakes and ocean, Mother Nature, and visits from his four children and five grandchildren.

Robert Mulligan

COURAGE

In a quiet place lives a voice, silent,
yet vibrant with energy

For what purpose, and to whom
does it speak

For courage and freedom from fear,
now, and for all to hear

There are times of light and
times of darkness

Times of fear yet times
of brightness

Always our choice, mine,
yours, all

WHY I WRITE

Where poetry breaks through the walls of logic,

defenses of the mind, and speaks directly to the heart

Here, I find solace from the structured sentence,

grammatical correctness, spelling, punctuation

So these words hit the page with a raw splash of emotion

uninhibited by the brain, as hand glides across the page.

Robert Mulligan

TEMPUS FUGIT

Being on-time
  And on-time being

Where minutes are money
  Each second calibrated at a fixed rate of return

And interest compounded daily
  Until we die

I carve out a small
  Space of timelessness

Watch it expand silently
  No hands moving, seconds ticking

Only changing patterns of light, dark
  Ambient cycles of being

Then timeless rest.

THE DAILY FOG

The day passes quickly but where was I

Seems I was somewhere else, my oh my

So hard to be present all of the time

Thinking of the future and what will be mine

As I watch the time pass without my presence

I know I am missing my life's essence

Lost in a fog of daily routine.

Robert Mulligan

THIS STEP

Following this footpath forward
    a gradual bend opens

To this peaceful plateau,
    a place to pause, rest

Offering a vista of past accomplishments,
    and distant disappointments

Ahead, gently sloping upward,
    a series of rises

Once a steep and challenging climb
    there were missteps, rockslides and setbacks

Here the passage becomes one of
    pleasure, reflection and wonder

Air clear and crisp, cleansing
    sun's rays brighter than I can remember

No summit to conquer, finish line to cross
    only this step, then the next.

INQUIRY

Better that life
    be an ongoing inquiry

Rather than mired
    in surety

Question more guiding
    than answer

Robert Mulligan

VICTORY

Of war, there is no winning

Last man standing, no victory

Offense, not a defense

Who started it first, a dance of denial

Fault lies alone in the willful destruction

Of irreplaceable resources, precious lives

The rent fabric of a society unmendable

But never a victor to be blamed.

THE EGO AT REST

Does the ego ever rest? Perhaps, or like the sleeping cat,
    always alert to every movement, sound

Prepared to pounce on each new opportunity
    displaying its agility, presence, superiority

Soul's silent sentry guarding the gateway
    to heartfelt connection

Yet spirit is no prisoner rather a patient witness
    awaiting the dissolving defenses no longer needed

And an opening and awakening
    of the soul

Robert Mulligan

KISSED BY A TREE

Twin trunked tree
Wind planted, or perhaps
A bird brought this seed to the fence line
Better to survive the sharp cutter blade

Now, in a field retired from active service
I ease this young sapling from its cramped dampness
Gently pressing its delicate network of fine roots
Into a warm, well drained site,
Feeding it with nutrients from well-aged compost
And, a prayer that it may grow tall and strong
It does

Years and seasons pass
I stop, on this clear cool evening
The moonless sky sparkles with diamonds
Placing my palms one on each trunk
I offer yet another prayer of gratitude
Wishing it many more years of well being

A gentle current runs through my arms
Coursing down through my body and into the ground
Muscles tremble from this unseen energy
Lovingly applied, and received
Unexplainable

Kissed by a tree.

Robert Mulligan

BIRTHDAY POEM

May your capacity to wish continue to grow
In each moment joy can flow
Ever… more fully

SEEKING SAMENESS

Seeking sameness
 Security, safety

Falsely feeling these familiar places
 Provide havens from risk of
  Disappointment, heartbreak

The bound foot of true passion

How does one grow in such a cramped cocoon
 Self-imposed restrictions, narrow boundaries

Experience the butterfly of your dreams
 No longer earthbound
  Fully trusting the vagaries of the wind.

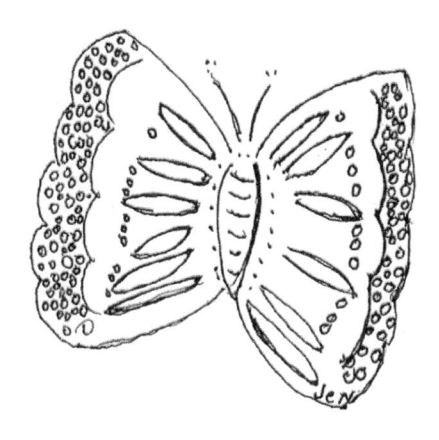

Robert Mulligan

MINUTE PARTICLES OF EXISTENCE

Measuring time in minutes, years
    Heartbeats and tears

Sunrises, sunsets
    Seasons of regrets

In minute particles
    Of existence

Life flows on.

DAYS UNTIL

Counting the days until………

The present moment a pleasant blur

Always an occasion to look forward to

And detailed planning keeps me "future focused"

A strong brew this mind-shaped reality

Robert Mulligan

EXHAUSTED OPTIONS

Recognize, this is about time defined
   In limiting seconds,….hours,…..years

    What compartments we do design
While boundless energy flows around us

       Timeless…..pleasure knows no such boundaries
And, what part does fear play in this equation

      Nature has but two positions
On, Off….Love, or Fear

       Choosing makes all the difference
Time, stands perfectly still

    Eternal,…Undefined…Waiting.

DISTANCE

It isn't the distance but the pleasure
   She smiled
      No goal to achieve
     Save joy
In that very instant
   Of presence
      Time ceases, measurement
       Becomes meaningless
For how does one gauge
   Fullness of life

      But in the depths of
     One's soul
The lightness of love
   In the heart
      And the meaning of existence
     In that moment.

Robert Mulligan

THE WRITTEN LETTER

Isn't it strange how hand-written letters seem
    More meaningful than those
Electronically composed bulletins

The richness of the ink inscribed on the paper,
    Each character drawn by a pen guided
By hand and heart

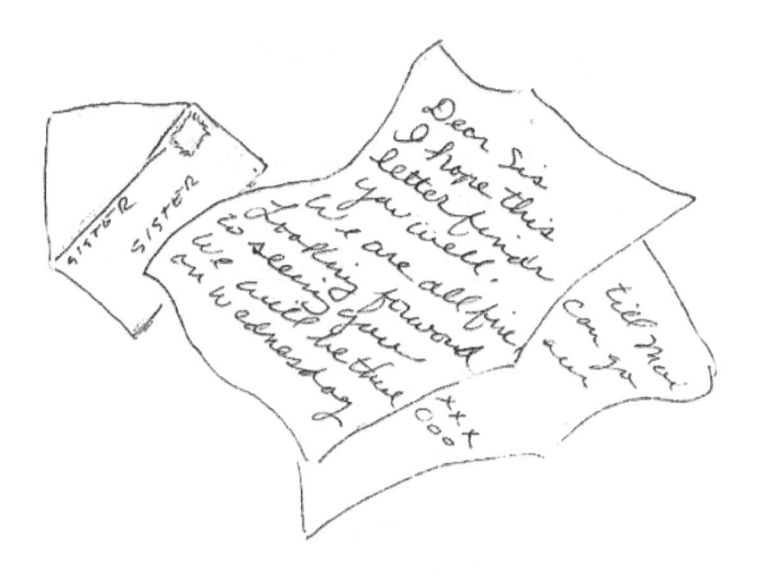

I save these gifts received from children now grown
    With families of their own, and grandchildren's
First attempts at writing their own name

Here, a drawer filled with letters from departed family members
    Post cards, scribbled notes on the back of pictures
Old friends, they revisit me, in the reading

Now, I step away from the computer, move to a seat at a table
    Pen and paper await. Writing slowly, more thoughtfully
There is no delete nor spell-checker function

Robert Mulligan

Next, the letter gets folded, inserted into an envelope and sealed,
    Leaving a minty flavor on my tongue. Addressing it brings an
Image of the receiver to mind, and the house it will arrive at

This small packet goes through many hands; sorted transported
    And delivered. One could question the economics of this
Outdated form of communication vs electronic transmission

The ancient tradition of hand delivered written messages has
    Survived for thousands of years, systems of transport reflecting
Mankind's history, this age may well be its final resting place

But in this moment, I picture my letter being opened, read
    Silently then aloud to other family members. They smile and many
miles away, I join them, feeling the warmth of this connection.

WHEN ONE WANTS IT ALL

How close to the fire
    Drawn by the flame of desire
This comforting warmth
    Becomes a funeral pyre

Hungry for bigger and better
    I inch closer to the edge
Just needing one more deal
    While nearing that precarious ledge

Are there winners and losers
    Who is to say?
Once the hook is set
    All come to know the blade

Robert Mulligan

NATURE

And the blizzards snow
    Rained down upon us
Sleet to freezing rain
    Back to snow

Nature said: "this too
    Is my season……
Just as yours turn from joyful
    Abundance to heartbreaking sorrow"

    *

Earth turning, emotions spinning,
    Moods of light, and dark
    *

Only ego sends us out into the storm
    From the warmth of our hearthstone
Proving our mastery of the elements
    Dominion over all God's creation

"Then this be my role"
    Nature reminds us with hurricane force
"My challenges be enough
    To temper you soul"

"Slacken your appetite for
    Self-destruction, war's devastation
May I be your only enemy
    If you choose"

"And when humility permits,
    Your ally, in peace and contentment."

Robert Mulligan

HOPE

*What **H**appens when all seems lost*

*You are **O**vercome by events beyond your control*

*But you **P**ersevere because you know that*

*That in the **E**nd all will be fine.*

    ***H**ow many times have you questioned*

    *The **O**utcome of a difficult situation*

    *Been **P**repared for the worst to occur only to find*

    *That **E**verything has turned out ok*

*They say **H**ope springs eternal*

*And **O**ne might find this true*

*When of all **P**ossible solutions*

***E**ach offers an opportunity to you*

    ***H**aving an open mind*

    *With **O**ptions to explore*

    *The **P**otential for success*

    ***E**xists for your hope to be restored*

B. Christa Kay

Christa is a native Mainer, born and raised in Brunswick. She is a graduate of Brunswick High School and attended the University of Maine.

Christa began freelance writing in 1987 and has been published in numerous periodicals including *The Times Record, The Kennebec Current, The Odyssey, The Sun Journal, The Critter Exchange* and *The Portland Press Herald*. Her writing experience includes desktop publishing of newsletters for various agencies and organizations. She has also created training manuals for non-profit agencies as well as corporate entities.

Christa has been an active volunteer in the community. She especially enjoys doing animal assisted therapy visits at area long term care facilities and assisting special needs children with therapeutic horseback riding for the Equine Special Olympics program. She has also volunteered at local animal shelters and wildlife rehabilitation centers.

B. Christa Kay

WHY I WRITE

The answer to that question is many fold.

I write because I enjoy the art of writing. Just like I enjoy reading a well-crafted prose, I enjoy the process of stringing words together in a coherent, interesting and meaningful way.

I write because I enjoy helping people tell their stories. There are so many interesting people, organizations and agencies doing wonderful things in our communities that I want to help them share their creations, endeavors and achievements with others.

I write because writing gives me some place to put my thoughts. The process of writing helps me sort things out.

I write because I enjoy sharing information.

I write because it is who I am.

B. Christa Kay

LUNCH WITH A SEAGULL

One afternoon several years ago I decided to lunch at a pretty little park in South Portland. I had anticipated a serene, uneventful dining experience but soon discovered that was not to be.

Within seconds after seating myself on a bench, I was joined by a flock of loud, hungry seagulls who settled themselves around me like ground fog, shattering my expectation of a quiet peaceful lunch. Being a lifelong Mainer, I was wise to the antics of these winged creatures and knew if I didn't give them anything to eat, they'd lose interest in me and fly off in search of a more accommodating luncheon patron.

Sure enough, within a few minutes a young boy carrying a McDonald's sack entered the park. As if on cue, the entire mass of birds erupted into the air and rushed to where the boy sat to see if they could mooch a morsel off him. Relieved, I returned my attention to my own lunch only to stop short after spying one lone seagull waiting expectantly just a few feet in front of my bench.

What was he still doing there I wondered? Why had he not flown off with the others? After all, I'd not given him anything to eat, nor did I intend to. Why was he still hanging around? I knew he could fly as I'd seen no seagulls near my bench prior to the flock's initial onslaught.

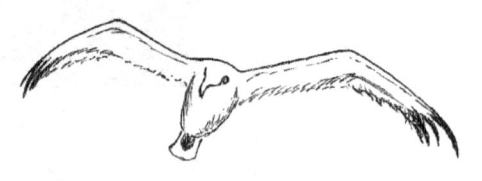

He was a smaller sized bird as seagulls go, certainly not the smallest in the park, but on the smaller size of average. He had the typical male seagull look; white body, light gray wings with black and white tips and a grayish beak with a strip of black and tipped in yellow. His white head was speckled with gray and his feet a greenish color and webbed. There appeared to be nothing unusual about this bird except his behavior. It seemed that something other than instinct motivated him. This gull was definitely different.

Although I'd had no intention of sharing my lunch with him or any other bird, I found this little gull's tenacity so astounding that I discreetly tossed him a piece of bread. I wasn't discreet enough, however, and within seconds the sky was again filled with flapping wings and screeching voices as the flock returned swarming down upon us.

This upset my feathered lunch mate who, for a moment, appeared overwhelmed by the commotion of the other birds settling in around him. Mouth wide agape, I watched as this incredible creature began to do, what I can only describe as, a war dance! Stamping his webbed feet and screaming, this little seagull tucked his head between his legs and then tossed it back up, pointing his beak skyward, to scream his anger for all to hear. Then with relentless determination he set about chasing away the encroachers who were trying to muscle in on his lunch. Not one bird fought with him or even fussed. Each just moved away and eventually, as other possible food sources entered the park, flew away to check out the contents of those lunch bags.

I wondered if I moved to another bench if this gull would follow me or if I would then be in another seagull's territory. Or perhaps this brassy little bird lay claim to the entire park! I brushed some chips to the ground near my feet to see just how bold this little bird really was. After staring intently at me with his yellow eyes he cautiously approached and as long as I didn't move, would come in, take a few pecks and move out to look at me again, then return for a few more bites and back away to where he could see me.

My logical mind set about trying to qualify this little gull's behavior. Apparently, this bird had been able to detach himself from the instinctual flock behavior of his species and developed his own unique method of eliciting food, which in this case had worked quite nicely!

I had long ago finished my lunch and shared with him all there was, yet still my winged friend remained. As I sat pondering the antics of this feathery fellow it occurred to me that maybe I could learn a thing or two. His independent and bold behavior spoke to me of individuality and courage and of the need to break free from the habitual "flocking" behavior of society.

It seemed this bird was suggesting that in order to discover my own personal method of emotional and spiritual nourishment I would do well to release those things I had been conditioned to believe and do. To discard the behavioral patterns that left me

B. Christa Kay

feeling empty and to seek out and develop the ones that filled and satisfied me.

As humans, perhaps the most difficult thing to do is to free ourselves from the need of having our personal healing style validated and accepted by other members of our "flock." The beauty of being human is the ability to act as individuals within our chosen religious tradition or support organization or social structure. It's an innate freedom; one we often forget we possess.

I was honored that this seagull had chosen to share his wisdom with me. His way of being in the world had not only won him some lunch, but had also earned him my respect. Perhaps this too was part of his teaching.

Previously Published in The Odyssey

A DOG'S LOVE

Shelby made someone's day this morning. Just by being herself.

We were out on our morning walk when a woman called to us from across a parking lot. She wanted to pat Shelby. She walked up to us with tears pouring from her eyes and explained that she'd had a Sheltie once whom she'd dearly loved and still missed although it had been six years since her Sheltie's passing. Her dog had died from complications of Lyme Disease.

Anyone who knows Shelties knows they can be a little standoffish when meeting new people. As the woman scooched down to pet my dog, Shelby walked right up to her, touching her nose to the woman's nose and gave the woman a little lick as if she knew the woman was upset.

As the woman cried and petted Shelby, she talked about her dog, Precious, and how she died and how much she was missed. She said she would never get another Sheltie because she'd already had the perfect one and no other Sheltie would ever compare to Precious. She told me that her next dog would be a different breed but that she was not yet ready to welcome another canine companion into her life.

I totally got it. I was glad she came over to us and asked to pet my dog. There is something special about the unconditional acceptance that is a dog's love. I can't imagine life without Shelby and I was happy to share her with this woman who was missing her dog, Precious

AUTUMN

While every season in Maine holds its own magic, I especially enjoy the magical season that is autumn.

As daylight shortens and temperatures cool
trees slowly bloom and gardens yield their final harvest.
Fat apples, bright orange pumpkins, jeweled ears of corn and strange looking squash are abundant. It is a time of family, feasts and festivals, of bon fires and ritual, of sweaters and hikes through a magically changing wood.

It is the season when maple trees, whose broad leaves previously provided a canopy of cooling shade, now offer a glorious spectacle of color; all yellow and red and orange and green.

B. Christa Kay

It is the season when plump orange pumpkins lend themselves to the carving of Jack-o-lanterns or to the making of pies; when apples, plucked ripe from the orchard, come home to simmer on the stove or bake in the oven and the scent of cinnamon lingers in the air.

It is the season which heralds change;
when leaves, having reached their full glory, loosen one by one then fly, tossed suddenly skyward on the autumn breeze briefly to dance and swirl then finally to rest on the cool fading green of the grass there to lend their beauty and warmth to the earth and their bodies to the soil.

The trees, now bare, remind us that winter is coming.

A CHRISTMAS MEMORY

There was snow that year at Christmas. Lots and lots of sparkly snow!! Best of all we were spending Christmas day at my aunt and uncle's house which sat at the top of a steeply slopped hill, perfect for sledding. I think I was more excited about the snow than I was about it being Christmas!!

After the gifts were exchanged and the dinner consumed, my brothers and I rushed outside bundled in one-piece snowsuits that zipped up the front and pinched the skin under my chin. We each had received a new set of hats, mufflers and mittens, hand knit by my aunt, for Christmas. Since I was still pretty young, my mittens came with a knitted cord attached that was long enough to go across the back of my neck and down both sleeves of my snowsuit so if my mittens came off while I was playing in the snow,

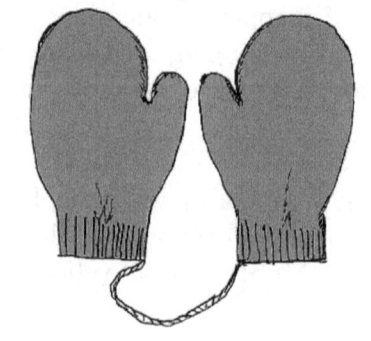

B. Christa Kay

I wouldn't lose them they'd just dangle from the cord at the end of my sleeve! My older brother's mittens didn't have that accessory which was kind of a right-of-passage in those days suggesting the owner possessed the necessary amount of responsibility to keep track of their mittens.

The air was cold, but we didn't feel it as we ran straight to the barn where we knew the sleds and toboggan waited. We soon discovered that the snow was too deep for sleds with runners but conditions were perfect for the long, wooden, flat bottomed, toboggan. My two older brothers were the first ones to ride it down the hill while my younger brother and I watched from the top of the hill in excited anticipation. The toboggan, in its downward trajectory, plowed through the deep powdery snow sending a wave of the cold stuff up and over the curved front of the toboggan. I could hear my two brothers laughing as they rolled off the sled. Turning, they looked back up the hill; their faces frosted white with snow while the cold of it painted their cheeks pink!!

Some of the adults had joined us at the top of the hill while others watched from a window. I could hear them laughing which made the sight even more comical. Grinning and wiping snow from their rosy faces, my brothers grabbed the toboggan rope and began the trek back up the hill, careful not to walk in the freshly blazed trail they had just made. When they reached the summit, they repositioned the toboggan and we all piled on. Down we went, again and again always trying to get the toboggan to slide just a bit further than the last time. It was great fun and we kept at it until our toes went numb and our fingers ached from the cold.

I have no memory of the gifts Santa brought that year. All I recall is the fun my brothers and I had sledding on that Christmas Day of the big snow!

B. Christa Kay

HALLOWEEN FROM MY WINDOW

From my second story apartment window I watch as local law enforcement work to set up grills and tables in the park across the street. Haunted music, seeping from giant speakers, create the perfect atmosphere for an evening of fun neighborhood Halloween festivities.

Next door, other worldly creatures appear, transforming empty lawns and drab driveways into spooky graveyards, haunted carnivals and scary arcades. Glowing Jack-o-lanterns guarding steps and grinning from windows welcome costume clad guests. White bone skeletons simmer in smoking black cauldrons while others gather around a table drinking beer and playing cards, their bony pets at their feet. Black clad witches stand by doorways ready to lose their cackling laugh at trick or treaters brave enough to knock for candy.

As the sun slowly slips below the horizon and shadows grow long under the streetlights outside my window, costumed creatures begin to swarm. Superheroes, dinosaurs, fairies, and monsters; witches, devils and angels, each grinning and clutching the handle of their steadily filling candy container, are eagerly shouting Trick-or-Treat as they go from place to spooky place.

As the sky grows darker it becomes harder to see what lurks on the streets below, but the sense of fun and excitement that carries up to my window reminds me of Halloweens' past and the fun I'd had.

TAKING A CHANCE

I wasn't sure I was ready to make the commitment. But when I thought about what life would be like with a constant companion, the fun we'd have, the places we'd go, the laughs we'd share, I decided to take a chance.

I perused many Facebook pages looking for just the right one. I saw so many pictures and tried to surmise what kind of companion each might be. In truth they all looked like they would make suitable companions. But how was I to truly know what kind of a companion they would be just by looking at a picture? Would we get along? Would they like my rabbits? Are they noisy and hyper or calm and cuddly? I'd never made a long-term commitment over the internet before. I narrowed my choice down to two possibilities; but how do I choose?

"Just pick one" she'd texted in answer to my query.

So, I did the only logical thing I could think of to do; I went eeny, meeny, miny, moe – the one I pick is you.

It's been two years and I can say that the chance I took that day turned out to be one of the best chances I've ever taken because it is how little Sebastian came to be my constant canine companion.

B. Christa Kay

WRITER'S BLOCK

How does one write when words evade capture
When thoughts dead end
When images fade into darkness

Holding a word in mind
I wait for inspiration to illuminate
the path on which I usually
discover a story to share

But not of late

Now it seems the words I try to hold
evaporate like mist
leaving me empty headed
with only nothingness inside

Granted, it's been a very long time
since I've tried to gather words
from the ethers,
to create a prose worth sharing

It's a worthy pursuit
so I shall continue to
search for that illusive path
to story

B. Christa Kay

COFFEE

Coffee, java, go juice
it's known by many names
Drip, percolated or pressed
It all turns out the same

Dark liquid hot and steaming
It's the only thing that stops me dreaming

First morning cup has got to be
A dark roast Arabica for me

Alene Staley

    Alene is a retired teacher who also worked as a school administrator and as a professional accountant. She has lived in Lisbon for the past 20 years and enjoys the access to trail systems and parks, and the community that she has found in the town.

    She enjoys writing and finds that the ***Write On Writers*** is a delightfully supportive group that helps to keep her writing interests alive. She was born in Chicago and lived in Virginia for ten years before moving to Maine. She loves Maine.

Alene Staley

AVIAN AND HUMAN NESTING HABITS

Nest is an almost perfect word. It is difficult to find a negative connotation for the word nest. Empty nest perhaps, but even that has a positive side. To nest is to make a home. To make it safe, durable, and comfortable.

Birds put great care and skill into building their nests. Many are only used once to raise young. Those that annually abandon nests explore new materials, designs and locations each year. Other birds such as eagles, osprey and herons use the same nests but do repairs and renovations to upgrade each spring.

Humans also nest. Some move around, some stay put. Nesting involves location, style, design, decoration and repair. If you read *Stranger in the Woods*, about Christopher Knight, the North Pond hermit, you will learn of his original and amazingly effective nesting skills. If you read *The Clan of the Cave Bear*, you will learn about the surprisingly complex nesting habits of ancient humans.

The current fashion trend in human nesting habits is to have moveable homes such as seen in the movie *Nomadland*. Another is to have tiny homes on wheels with clever storage systems, and to locate them close to nature in scenic places. These trends have replaced a previous nesting style which was to build large homes in suburbs.

I wonder if birds are as interested in human nesting habits as humans are interested in bird nesting habits.

Alene Staley

CHIPMUNKS

Chipmunks deserve respect. Humans are thought to have evolved five to seven million years ago. Seventy million years ago squirrels evolved from the rodent family and soon chipmunks, with their distinctive stripes and adorable cheeks, evolved from the squirrel family. After all, we humans are the new kids on the block.

When I lived in Virginia, we had two cats. The house was located in an area with many trees. Wherever there are nut bearing trees, there are chipmunks. Chipmunks do not casually wander into a house. Cats bring them inside. It takes only a short second for a cat to bring a chipmunk inside and release it. It is extremely difficult for a human to capture and rescue a chipmunk. Of course, you could let a cat catch the chipmunk for you, but could you trust the cat?

Chipmunks have two strategies when threatened, playing dead and hiding. We discovered that if you left shoes around the living room, and kept a close eye on the chipmunk, eventually it would crawl into a shoe. We would quickly toss the shoe outside without letting any cats escape. After about ten minutes we would go out and check the shoe. Sometimes we would have to shake it gently to encourage the chipmunk to come out.

So, I ask you. Considering humans, cats, and chipmunks, who are the most highly evolved? Who are the smartest?

Alene Staley

MY WALDEN

I enjoy walking in the woods. I always have found pleasant natural environments where I could regularly visit to recharge, relax, contemplate, and of course, exercise. Upon moving to Lisbon twenty years ago I discovered Beaver Park.

The park has three ponds, stocked with fish, and 35 miles of groomed trails. Two picnic shelters host wedding parties, reunions, graduation and birthday parties. Picnic areas are available through the park which is open year around.

Like many people, I go there to walk on the well-marked nature trails. In the spring, wildflowers, including lady slippers, trailing arbutus, clintonia, and starflowers are abundant. In the summer, great blue heron are regular visitors as are ducks and geese. In winter, trails are groomed for cross country skiing and snowshoeing. The ponds are cleared for skating.

I enjoy a nice long hike, some bird watching, checking out what is blooming, watching dragonflies, butterflies, turtles and frogs. Then I like to sit for a while and enjoy the tranquility. Oh, and of course, a pleasant conversation along the way makes it perfect.

Alene Staley

MUSING ABOUT COPYING

    We humans think that we are rational beings that function with reason and are not guided by instinct. When we look at animals, we see instinct not rationality. I wonder if we are missing something.

    According to PBS some baby ducks have to step off the edge of their nest which is high in a tall tree, and drop many feet to a leaf bed to follow their mother to the pond. This we see as instinct. Have you ever seen a kitten leaping and pouncing at play? You can clearly see they know how to catch prey without being taught. It's instinct. Turtle eggs are left in the nest while turtle mothers return to the sea. New born baby turtles know to go as fast as possible to the water when they hatch. Again instinct.

    But what about us humans? I suggest there is a human behavior that we know very early. We use it constantly. No one teaches it to us. And we share this behavior with other animals. The behavior is copying the behavior of other humans. Babies learn to talk by copying their parents. They learn to walk by copying their family. Almost everything humans do involves copying. Our ability to copy each other is perhaps our most important human skill. But how do we learn how to copy? Might it be that copying is a human instinct?

    We recently experienced the rapid development of vaccines to fight Covid-19, an amazing accomplishment. It happened because scientists used work previously done by others and modified it to fight a new threat. The success resulted from a complex web of copying and modifying. So, I ask, "Are humans the most advanced 'copier' species?" Is copying behavior a human instinct?

Alene Staley

A ONE-SIDED NARRATIVE FROM THE TIME BEFORE CELL PHONES

"So what do you think Tom? We could go to the front of the building. It would take at least twenty minutes to get to the ground level with everyone heading out for the weekend, or we could take the freight elevator. What do you think? I don't think there are any rules against it. There is no warning sign. We could push the button and see if anything is loaded or if there is anyone heading down. See if it's empty."

"I'll just push the button. Here it is. It looks empty. Are you going to join me? That's good. Do you think the loading dock is B-1? Let's try it. Gee, that was fast. Any idea why the door isn't opening?"

(Two hours later.)

"Gee I'm sorry Tom. Who could imagine that you could get stuck in an elevator in a federal building on a Friday afternoon, and no one seems to hear the emergency alarm, and why isn't there a phone in here? Do you think your wife will be worried?"

(Loud Banging.)

"We're opening the door. Stay back. You're going to have to climb out. We can't get the elevator to the floor level. By the way, it's not a good idea to take the freight elevator. You will have to go out the front door and check with security. Take the stairs."

HOPE RETURNED

Hope is spring warmth drawing us outside.
That which held us in its grip shifts, arcing wide,
To fly afar and disappear.
While Joy, and Peace, and Deep Breath reappear.
We sing of sweet relief and memory and hope.
Dread and fear replaced by power to cope.
Remembering the truth of lessons endured,
We relish Love and Joy and Hope returned.

Alene Staley

A SPECIAL GARDEN IN A SECRET PLACE

There is a special garden in a secret place where only members of an elite club may go. To enter the garden, you must go through a small structure, then open a screen door and walk out into the garden. What makes this garden so special is that all the flowering plants are blue. All different shades of blue. Tall flowers, short flowers, creeping plants and vines all blue with green leaves. There is a stream that comes from a nearby natural spring that continuously provides clear fresh water to the garden. If you want to find this secret garden, you must join a club. Most people in this club are under twelve years old. The members love to swing at the park. They swing as high as they can. When they reach the highest point before the swing falls back towards the ground, if they look straight ahead, they can see the special garden, and they know exactly how to get there.

THE IMPORTANCE OF SMILES IN MY DAY

A stranger smiling at me is a wonderful gift. Smiling at strangers makes me happy. I suppose you could make the case that smiling at strangers is risky, but in my over seven decades of life I have found no evidence that is true. I have had deep sadness in life at times, as has everyone. For me walking is always the best way to cope. Walkers regularly smile at each other. Sometimes just one smile was all I needed to get through a difficult day. Isn't it absolutely a miracle that something so easy and completely free, is perfect.

Made in the USA
Middletown, DE
14 October 2022